The Millennial Playbook

9 Secrets To Living A Rich Life

Raphael Enrique Collazo

The Millennial Playbook: 9 Secrets To Living A Rich Life
Copyright © 2018 by Raphael Enrique Collazo

All rights reserved. No part of this book may be reproduced or transmitted in any form or by any means without written permission from the author.

ISBN 978-0-9993348-1-2

Printed in the USA by CreateSpace

What people are saying about
The Millennial Playbook

"Over the course of my 20-year career as a professional keynote speaker, coach and best-selling author I have read many self-books and met many of the most influential speakers in the self-help industry. Through it all, I've drawn lessons from these individuals and shared these insights with the world. I loved how Raphael was able to share many of these same lessons into actionable content Millennials can use to improve their life for the better."

-Patrick Snow
International Best-Selling Author, Coach
and Professional Keynote Speaker

"Raphael Collazo does a great job breaking down important concepts for development and life success, not only for Millennials but for anyone reading this book. The book includes stories and research to back up the easily understood concepts. Action items and additional resources make this a valuable book for anyone looking to get ahead in life. This would be a great high school or college graduation gift!"

-Dr. Karen Kramer
International Success Advocate and
Life Coach for Teens and 20-Somethings

This is a fantastic read for anyone who wants to become their best self and be better than the day before. I've read my fair share of self-help books over the course of my life and wish I'd read this book years ago!"

Kristy Vee,
Reader's Favorite

"The Millennial Playbook is a must read for this generation to succeed both personally and professionally. As a licensed psychotherapist for over 20 years, I can verify that the tools and skills outlined in this book are well researched, clinically sound, easily understood and practical for anyone wanting to live their best life. I highly recommend this book to anyone wanting to take life to the next level."

-Elisabeth Caetano MA
Author of *Down the Rabbit Hole and Back*

"Raphael uses his personal experiences, the mistakes he's made, the challenges he's had to overcome, the battles he's won, and the lessons he's learned along the way to offer a comprehensive guide to fellow Millennials."

-FAIDAH NASSOZI
Readers' Favorite

"In The Millennial Playbook, *Raphael has done an excellent job distilling pertinent and ACTIONABLE information. What separates this book, in my opinion, is how it's rooted in practicality."*

– J.P Melanson
Millennial financial planner

"With so many lists on the internet providing what they proclaim to be important info for Millennials, this book distills great insights and provides actionable challenges that are valuable to anyone looking to improve their lives!"

– Ryan Sariego
Millennial Operations manager

"This book takes the fundamentals of success for a young professional and breaks them down to an understandable level I've not seen elsewhere. It takes ideas young people are expected to know, but were never actually taught, and lays them out clearly so the reader can begin to build on the concepts. I'll be recommending to all my friends."

-Joe Zurek
Millennial Healthcare Operations Associate

"This book is filled with helpful strategies and tips you can implement right away in your day-to-day life. Since we're close to the new year, I found the 'goal setting' section extremely useful. I'm definitely going to be using the S.M.A.R.T. goal setting technique as I write out my New Year's resolutions!"

– Damon Drayfahl
Amazon Review

"This is an excellent book. I agree 100% with all that's been said in the 5-star reviews. The guidance that Raphael Collazo shares is practical and inspiring. His writing is personable. This book would be a great addition to gift giving at college graduation time."

-Hiker04
Amazon Review

"Excellent book, quick read, and tons of great suggestions on ways to improve your life. This book not only helped me in my personal development but other areas as well. Everything you need to know is in this easy to read book. Highly recommended."

-Melanie Rivera
Amazon Review

Dedication

Wow, what a journey it's been. I would have never thought that within one year I'd be able write two books that have impacted so many lives around the world. The hundreds of early morning writing sessions, the countless hours of editing, and the struggle of fighting through consistent writer's block have been worth it. All the proceeds of my previous book, *The Millennial Playbook,* were donated to hurricane relief efforts in Puerto Rico. As a result, we were able to raise over $1,000 in donations for the Ricky Martin Foundation. The foundation has and continues to do a phenomenal job supporting recovery efforts on the island. For those of you who have purchased the book, thank you for making a significant impact on someone else's life. If you have yet to purchase the book, it's not too late! I've provided a link to the book here: (https://www.amazon.com/Millennial-Playbook-Success-Strategies-Generation/dp/0999334808).

As in the previous book, I want to thank my beautiful, confident, and inspiring girlfriend Melanie. Without your constant support and review of my work, I would have never completed this book. I'd also like to thank my family for their guidance and love throughout the years. You've instilled the confidence, knowledge, and love that I'll need to ensure my success in life. Finally, I'd like to thank you, my readers, for your constant support of my work and your messages of success and hope. You're the reason why I write and will continue to write in the future.

All the best,

Raphael Collazo

Contents

Preface

My journey with writing began on Mar 15, 2015. It was the day I received a poor quarterly review from my project manager. I remember feeling completely crushed and utterly confused about what I should do in response. The year prior I'd been working as a restaurant manager and building my pasta catering business in Phoenix, Arizona. It was a period of exploration and growth that shaped me into the man I am today. However, for much of that time and some time thereafter, I had no idea what I wanted to do with my life. Every day I'd wake up and question why I was doing what I was doing. I believed there was something bigger in store for me. Fast forward one year, and I had just received an offer for an implementation consultant role at a mid-size software consulting firm. During my first three months, I struggled to acclimate and was even considering quitting to move back home. When my boss gave me the negative review, the option to quit seemed very appealing.

However, before I made my decision, I decided to write out the pros and cons of each decision. I took out a piece of paper, marked *March 15, 2015,* at the top of the page, and began to write. As I evaluated the possible scenarios, I began to feel a sense of relief. Writing out my feelings put the situation into perspective. I was not being told I wasn't good enough; I was being challenged to do better. That day I decided to respond to my project manager's evaluation by doubling down my efforts.

As the months progressed and my performance improved, I continued to write about topics that interested me. In July 2016 I created my blog, *The Strong Professional*, to share the articles I'd been writing with the world. The positive response I received from these articles was immediate, and I began contemplating how I could provide a more comprehensive version of the lessons I'd been sharing. This is where the inspiration for *The Millennial Playbook* series came to be. You're now reading the second book in the series, which focuses on topics related to the first pillar of living a fulfilling life: *Personal Development.* In this book, you'll learn unique and actionable strategies you can use to chart a course to a better life. Because of my desire to provide the most useful strategies, I've spent countless hours researching to ensure that these strategies are deeply rooted in science. I've also provided action items at the end of each section to make it easier for you to implement them into your own life. I hope this book helps change the way you view the world, and I'd love to hear your stories of success!

Introduction

Before we delve too far into the book, it's important to understand who this book is intended for. So, who are the Millennials? We are individuals born between the years of 1982 and 2000. We've often been described as the tech savvy generation due to our upbringing around technology. With approximately 83 million Millennials living and working in the United States, we make up about one-quarter of the US population. Our generation is filled with bright, driven, innovative people who want to make a positive impact on the world.

Along with these positive traits, we also have some less favorable ones. Since we've grown up in a world where technology has made everything around us easier to access and process, we tend to seek immediate gratification in almost every endeavor we pursue. This is true in both our personal and professional lives. It's common to see Millennials feeling discouraged because they're not making an immediate impact in an organization. Social media also plays a big role in our day to day lives. The average US Millennial has five social media accounts and spends an average of one hour and forty minutes daily maintaining them.[31] This has affected many Millennials who are looking to build and maintain long-term romantic relationships.

Based on this profile, the question then becomes: How do we go about improving the areas of our life that fall into these negative categories while maintaining the positive characteristics that make our generation one that will make a lasting positive impact on the world? Throughout the rest of this book, I seek to answer this question. Through concepts I've learned from some of the most successful and inspiring thought leaders of our time, I've compiled a manuscript of some of the best concepts we as Millennials can apply to improve our lives. In this book, you'll learn about how choices impact your long-term success, how to develop a winning mindset, how to achieve long-term happiness, how to build personal relationships, how to bookend your days, and how to build confidence and continue your education over time. These concepts make up the core of my personal development philosophy and can be applied to achieve fantastic results.

This book is not for the faint of heart and those easily deterred by life's obstacles and challenges. This book is not for the complainers and whiners who view life as being unfair or unjust. This book IS for the doers and thinkers of our generation. Those of us willing to answer the call and sacrifice to improve each and every day. If you adhere to the former viewpoint, you need not read further. This book is not for you. However, if you aspire to the latter viewpoint, this will be your new playbook, your guide to charting a course to a better life. Are you ready to dive in and explore these wonderful concepts that can change your life forever? If so, let's begin.

Chapter 1
The choices you make

◆

"Everything in life is a reflection of the choices you've made. If you want a different result, start making different choices." – Unknown

What's the one defining factor that's brought you to this point in life? What's responsible for your current health, wealth, relationships, and career? All these areas of your life have one thing in common. They're a result of all the CHOICES you've made up to this point in time. Now, these are generally not massive, life altering decisions. After all, people don't become obese from eating one bag of chips, don't ruin their relationships by missing one family dinner, and don't go broke by deciding to buy that latte before work. It's a summation of all the small choices they make day to day that result in their current situation. If you're unhappy with any area of your life, you need to modify the choices you make on a day to day basis.

But before we start looking at what choices to modify, we must first address how you view your choices. I always find it surprising when people blame others for the poor decisions they make. When a person complains about how they don't have time to go to the gym, they never want to address the fact that they watch Netflix for three hours when they get home from work. When a person blames the government for their bad financial situation, they never want to address the countless useless items they've purchased over time that have dwindled their savings. When a person blames his/her boss or a coworker for not receiving a promotion, they never want to address the fact that they leave work at 5 p.m. every day and never go the extra mile to help others at work. We tend to have a rosy view of ourselves and find it difficult to objectively judge our situation in life.

In order to make the changes necessary to improve your life, you'll first need to learn how to take 100% responsibility for your actions. If you don't have the body you desire, take responsibility for your prior decisions and make the commitment to implement an exercise regimen and healthy diet into your routine. If you don't have the relationships you desire, own your previous shortcomings and commit to being more attentive to your partner and focusing on improving communication. If you don't have the financial wellbeing you desire, acknowledge your poor spending habits and commit to saving more money each month or dedicating the necessary time to start a side business to make extra money. All these choices, whether good or bad, will add up to your future life. Although you may be upset with your current situation, don't get down in the dumps over it. It's never too late to stop making negative choices and switch to making positive ones. Each positive choice you make from this point forward will help you build momentum and eventually provide the breakthrough you need to change your life.

In the book *The Compound Effect*, Darren Hardy encourages his readers to carry around a journal to log the choices they make in a particular focus area throughout the day. For example, if you wanted to increase the amount you saved each month, you would write down every penny you spend for an entire week. Oftentimes we forget how small purchases can add up to LARGE expenses over time. One of the statistics mentioned in Darren's book states that if you apply an 8% yearly rate of return, $1 spent today is worth $5 in 20 years and $10 in 30 years. Knowing this, you may find it easier to abstain from buying that $4 latte each morning. This method can be applied to various areas of your life, including healthy eating habits (write down everything you eat during the day); building better relationships (write down every time you do or say something positive/negative to your significant other); your personal development (write down three things you're grateful for each day);

etc. By performing this exercise, you'll see how the small choices you make every day begin to add up.

Once you finish the one-week challenge, sit down and review your results. Are you surprised with what you see? I know that when I did this exercise for my finances, I was shocked with how little expenses added up for me. Now that you've become more aware of the choices you make on a day to day basis, try performing this exercise for another two weeks. According to Aubrey Daniels, often referred to as "the father of performance management," you need at least 300 instances of positive reinforcement to solidify a new positive habit.[19] By extending the amount of time you track your results, you'll get ever closer to reaching that magic number. Not only that, but I remember that by the end of my tracking period, I would consciously avoid purchasing items because I didn't want to pull out my journal to log the purchase. Try this exercise out for yourself and see what a difference it makes. Now that you understand the role that making the right choices has on your day to day life, let's delve into how to develop a winning psychology so you can get into the right mindset for success.

Chapter 2
Developing a winning psychology

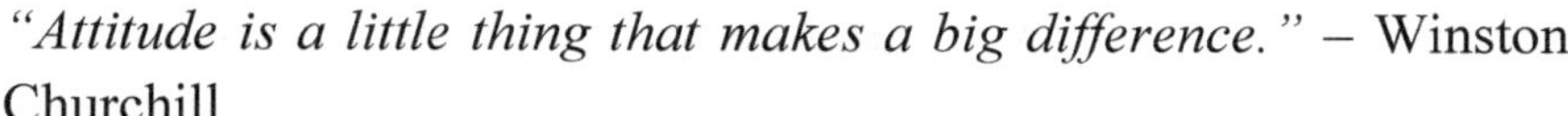

"Attitude is a little thing that makes a big difference." – Winston Churchill

The beginning of every personal growth journey starts with developing a winning psychology. What do I mean by this? I mean you must first open your mind to the idea of adopting positive habits and routines. A farmer must first ensure the soil is fertile before he/she plants the seeds that will eventually grow into bountiful crops. If the soil is rocky, dry, or lacks the proper minerals, nothing will grow there. In other words, it doesn't matter how many new and positive ideas you hear if your mind is not ready to accept and act upon them. If this step is ignored, you can expect to regress back to your old ways in no time. So what actions can you take today to ensure that you establish a positive and winning mindset? Let's go over some of the best techniques:

The importance of a positive attitude

As we approach our day to day activities, it's important to keep a positive outlook on life. There will be days where everything seems to be working against you. As a result, you may feel negatively about your situation. However, if you're constantly engaging in negative thoughts, they will manifest themselves into negative experiences. One such negative experience happened to me when I was fired from my job as a server. After college graduation, I decided to work full-time on the business venture I started with a friend in college. It was a pasta catering company named "Pasticity," and we had experienced some success my junior and senior year. As I worked to grow the business, I also worked as a server at a local fast casual dining restaurant near downtown Phoenix. Over the next eight months, I tried unsuccessfully to stir up interest in my business and didn't generate much in the way of revenue. All the while, I was working at the restaurant to help pay the bills. The more my business began to waver, the more my confidence faltered and my attitude became increasingly negative and pessimistic. When I finally realized that owning a restaurant was not my passion, I closed the business and diluted what little assets I had.

After closing operations, I fell into a negative funk. Every day seemed worse than the last, and I kept thinking about how I had wasted almost a year of my life pursuing something that didn't work out. This was the first time in my life that I had experienced a sizable failure, and I didn't handle it well. As my attitude began to deteriorate, so did my work performance. I got complacent at work and began making mistakes. One mistake in particular cost the restaurant over $200. I botched a large catering order and had to reimburse the client 50% of the purchase price. My humiliation at this event further compounded my negative attitude and within a month, I was fired from the restaurant.

After the firing, I went home, sat on my couch, and stared blankly into space for a while. What was I going to do now? After taking some time to run through the last few months in my mind, I realized that the common thread in all my troubles was my negative attitude. I decided then I needed to adopt a more positive outlook on life and began working towards improving. Through hard work, diligence, and a positive disposition, I was able to land a well-paying consulting role at a software development company that has afforded me the opportunity to live and work in Washington DC, Puerto Rico, and Louisville. Now, I'm not saying it was an easy road to employment. Over the course of four months, I was rejected by more than 10 different employers before landing my current role. However, if I hadn't maintained a positive attitude through these rejections, I'm confident I wouldn't have continued to push myself to find new opportunities. Take some time this week to evaluate your attitude. Do you have a negative disposition? If so, commit to eliminating it immediately. A negative attitude will hold you back from achieving your goals and living the life you desire.

The little voice inside your head

Oftentimes I feel as though there's a little man living inside my head. This man can be insidious and often directs hurtful words and phrases at me. There are times when I let this little man get to me and I fall into a negative funk. However, whenever I choose to acknowledge his negativity and move past it, I find that my mind is clearer and I'm much more productive throughout the day. In reality, this little man is the culmination of all the negative thoughts inside your head. Whenever things don't go your way, it can be easy to blame it on yourself and feel bad about your situation. One of the best ways to get out of this funk is to replace those negative thoughts with words of positivity and encouragement.

In a meta-analysis led by Antonis Hatzigeorgiadis at the University of Thessaly, he and his colleagues sought to discover whether "self-talk" improved athletes' performance in various activities. The results showed that for athletes who focused on improving fine motor skills and movements, "instructional self-talk" was the most effective. Examples of this kind of self-talk include telling yourself to *"keep your chest up and your shoulders back"* when performing a squat or to *"keep your elbow in"* as you swing a baseball bat. However, for athletes who performed feats of strength and endurance, "motivational self-talk" was the most effective. Examples of this kind of self-talk includes phrases such as *"you can do it"* or *"give it your all."* This kind of self-talk had the effect of boosting confidence and psyching up competitors before their respective competitive events.[18]

You don't have to be an Olympic athlete to benefit from positive self-talk either. What I often do when I'm feeling down is tell myself how awesome I am and how resilient I can be in the face of adversity. Over time, I've been able to change my default beliefs, and I'm now extremely confident in my abilities. Another exercise I recommend to my clients is to write out the limiting beliefs they've been harboring. Examples of these beliefs include phrases such as, *"I'm stupid and can't get anything right," "I'm ugly and no one will ever love me," "I'm fat and I'll always struggle with my weight," and "I'm poor and I'll never have the nice things I want in life."*

These limiting beliefs are holding you back from achieving your goals and need to be eliminated from your vocabulary. It's crucial that you replace these negative phrases with new positive ones. Examples of these phrases may include, *"I'm intelligent and can make something of myself," "I'm pretty as hell and people love me," "I'm lean, sexy, and ready for action," "I live a rich and abundant life full of wealth and prosperity."* Repeating these new positive affirmations will slowly change your default beliefs and transform your reality into a positive one. Try this technique out for yourself and see how well it works for you.

Battling your subconscious beliefs

Have you ever really wanted something (money, love, happiness, etc.) but no matter how hard you tried to achieve it, it never seemed to come to fruition? If you answered "yes" to this question, you may be interested in learning how your subconscious beliefs impact your day to day life. Sigmund Freud, the famous German psychoanalyst and researcher, highlighted the principles of the conscious and subconscious minds in his paper titled, *"The Ego and the Id."* In the paper, Freud discusses three distinct parts of an individual's personality. These are the Ego, the Superego, and the Id.

The Id is the oldest part of your personality and is present at birth. Freud describes it as the *"the dark, inaccessible part of your personality"* whose only concern is to seek pleasure and avoid pain. Therefore, this part of your subconscious mind has no judgement of value. To give you a real-world example, the Id is the part of your personality telling you to devour that chocolate cake when you see it in front of you.

The Superego is the other part of your subconscious mind that develops as you learn and grow. It's often considered the opposite of the Id because it's the part of our brain that controls our sense of right vs. wrong. External influencers, especially those in positions of authority, play a pivotal role in the development of your Superego. Your parents are the first people to mold your Superego as they teach you what they consider right and wrong. As a result, this is the part of our brain that helps us conform to society and adopt societal norms. Going back to the cake example, this is the part of your brain telling you that eating the chocolate cake is bad and that you'd be a terrible person for eating it.

Finally, the Ego is the conscious part of your personality. This is the part of your personality where your common sense and reasoning lives. It enables you to organize your thoughts and use them to make judgements on the external world. As your Id and Superego battle it out to influence your decision, your Ego is objectively looking at the situation and drawing its own conclusions. As it relates to the chocolate cake example, this would be the part of your personality that would either indulge or deny the cake, depending on the rationale behind the decision. Freud often likened the relationship between the Ego and the subconscious mind *as "a man on horseback who has to hold in check the superior strength of the horse."* Since your subconscious mind is often much stronger than your conscious mind, your Ego can be easily influenced by these parts. Therefore, learning how to balance all three parts of your personality will help you achieve your desires in life.[50]

Now that you understand each part of your personality, let's explore how you can modify your subconscious mind to better support your goals and aspirations. Your Superego is the part of your mind where your efforts can have the most impact. Many of us have limiting beliefs that have been drilled into us for many years. Oftentimes what happens is that our parents, out of love and a desire to protect us, dampen our beliefs and desires. You may have wanted to pursue a career in acting, but your parents may have told you that only bums pursue acting careers and that you should become a lawyer instead. This may lead you to abandoning your pursuit of an acting career and instead opting to go to law school to satisfy your parents' wishes. Another example may be that your loved ones were constantly struggling financially and always stressed the mantra that *"money doesn't grow on trees."* Therefore, you associate the acquisition of money as a negative thing and perpetuate this negative belief throughout your life; thus, never attaining financial freedom.

Joseph Goebbels, the Nazi propaganda minister, often said, *"If you tell a lie big enough and keep repeating it, people will eventually come to believe it."* The lies in this case are the limiting beliefs you've been conditioned to adhere to by external influences. In order to break free of these limiting beliefs, you must replace them with positive beliefs. Come up with an idea for something you want to do and repeat it to yourself until you believe it. This may take some time, but if you say it often enough and long enough, your subconscious (Superego) will begin to respond.

Beware of moral licensing

Have you ever worked out or eaten a healthy meal and used it as justification to eat a few donuts or skip a few workouts later in the week? If you answered "yes" to this question, you've borne witness to the power of "moral licensing." Moral licensing is a subconscious phenomenon whereby *"someone's increased confidence and security in their self-image or self-concept makes them worry less about the consequences of subsequent immoral behavior and, therefore, more likely to make immoral choices and act immorally.* "[54] In other words, we often justify our negative behavior by referring to our positive self-image. Although it's important to have a positive self-image, using it to justify immoral actions can get you into deep water. Recent studies have shown just how detrimental moral licensing can be in our lives.

In a 2011 paper published by researchers in Taiwan, the researchers analyzed the effects taking multivitamins had on people's decision-making. At the beginning of the study, each group was given placebo pills. The first group was informed that the pills were in fact placebos while the second was told that the pills were multivitamin supplements. After a few weeks of taking the placebos, each group was administered a survey. The results showed that participants in the multivitamins group were predisposed to smoke more cigarettes and more likely to believe they were invulnerable to harm, injury, and disease when compared with those in the placebo group. They were also less likely to exercise or choose healthier meals and were more likely to engage in *"hedonic activities that involve instant gratification but pose long-term health hazards"* such as casual sex, sunbathing, excessive drinking, etc.[55] If you're struck by the absurdity of these results, it's not even the tip of the iceberg.

In an article published by a team of professors at the University of Oxford, the professors sought to uncover how the mere presence of healthy options affected our decision-making. In the article, the professors reference how McDonalds' Big Mac sales skyrocketed after they added healthier options to their menu. Although people around the United States and the world were clamoring for healthier options on the menu, they actually weren't eating them! The mere fact that healthy options were on the menu gave their customers justification to indulge in their favorite greasy and unhealthy options.[56]

Conditioning ourselves to avoid these negative behaviors is crucial if we want to make positive changes in our lives. Start by acknowledging that your mind will try to justify negative behaviors. Whenever you're about to make a seemingly bad decision, ask yourself these two questions: *"Is this the best decision for me to make?"* and *"Would I make this same decision if I hadn't done something positive in the past?"* If you answered "no" to either of these questions, it may be an indication that you should avoid the action altogether. Now that we've talked about how to condition yourself to better respond to positive influences, let's delve into how you can restrict negativity from invading and polluting your mind.

Garbage in, garbage out

"Every day, stand guard at the door of your mind, and you alone decide what thoughts and beliefs you let into your life. For they will shape whether you feel rich or poor, cursed or blessed." – Jim Rohn

A few months after graduating from college, I came across some YouTube videos of Jim Rohn, a personal development guru who mentored the likes of Tony Robbins, Darren Hardy, and many other titans of the personal development industry. His lessons were simple yet practical and when I applied them, I experienced significant improvement in various areas of my life. One of my favorite lessons is the concept of *"garbage in, garbage out."* The idea is that if you consistently consume negative and pointless content, you'll inevitably get bogged down in this reality. Reading tabloids, listening to negative media, and gossiping about others are just a few examples of stimuli that can leave you in a negative mental state. In order to maintain a positive mindset, it's imperative that you eliminate these influences from your life. In this section, we'll go over some of the actions you should avoid.

Eliminating negative news channels

I'm often frustrated by the negativity of the media today. Every time I turn on Fox News, CNN, MSNBC, and many other news outlets, I can't help but notice all the negative and apocalyptic messages broadcast to viewers around the world. I consistently see stories about wars in other parts of the world, nuclear threats, terrorist attacks, serial killers on the loose, and many other topics that spread a message of negativity, hate, and intolerance. Although my heart breaks for the families of those affected by these terrible acts, there are also many beautiful and wonderful things happening around the world each and every day. People helping one another after severe storms, a person escaping abject poverty to become the first in his/her family to attend college, a recovering drug/alcohol addict who overcomes his addiction and is now helping others do the same. These examples and many others like them are often thrown by the wayside in favor of more shocking and violent stories.

Although this is the case, we can't blame the media entirely. We instigate this behavior by engaging in their negative rhetoric. In a study conducted by McGill University professors Marc Trussler and Stuart Soroka, the professors invited university students to their lab for an eye tracking study. In the study, participants were told to select and read articles from a political site while their eye movement was tracked. At the end of the allotted time, the participants were shown a short video that asked them what kind of political articles they liked to read. The results of the study showed that participants often gravitated towards stories with negative tones, corruption, setbacks, and hypocrisy. Not only that, people who were more interested in current affairs and politics were particularly more likely to choose the bad news.[11]

This is what is known as a "negativity bias" and it causes many of us to gravitate towards negative news. Instead of filling your mind with negative media, try following positive and uplifting news. In a study conducted by Dr. Barbara L. Frederickson, Dr.

Frederickson analyzed groups of people as they were exposed to positive content and tracked how it affected their creativity and social interactions. At the end of the study, participants who were exposed to positive content reported having a happier disposition than those who were exposed to negative content. Not only that, participants who engaged with positive content were more creative, better able to interact in a social setting, and developed various skills quicker than participants who experienced negative emotions from negative content.[12] These insights have led me to only engage with news that focuses on topics relevant to my industry, content that helps me expand my skill set, and/or content that provides a motivational and uplifting message.

One of the only newsletters I'm subscribed to is "Morning Brew". Each morning, I receive a newsletter highlighting the financial market activity for the previous day as well as other financial related news. I love how they're able to offer unique and insightful information in a fun and concise manner. I highly recommend the newsletter and have provided a link to subscribe here: www.morningbrew.com

By only engaging with news that meets my criteria, I'm able to abstain from negative media and keep my mind free of negative messages that cloud my mind. Try going on a negative news fast yourself and see how much more positive and engaged you feel throughout the day.

Reducing social media exposure

As Millennials, social media is as much a part of our lives as watching television was to previous generations. From the days of Myspace, to now Facebook, Twitter, Instagram, LinkedIn, Pinterest, and everything in between, we're constantly being bombarded with stimuli and demands for our attention. This problem is only compounded by the fact that we can download these social media apps to our phone and carry them with us throughout the day.

Although social media can be a powerful tool to grow your network and expand your audience, it also has a dark side. Researchers at Nottingham Trent University coined the phrase "Facebook Addiction Disorder" to describe a condition experienced by some study participants who used social media excessively. These participants showed signs of addiction such as neglect of their personal life, mental preoccupation, escapism, mood modifying experiences, tolerance, and concealing their addictive behavior.[51] Photos of your friends' "perfect" lives on Facebook and Instagram feeds can make you feel like you have to compete with them to show off how great your life is. In results from one study published in the *Journal of Social and Clinical Phycology*, researchers discovered a positive correlation between time spent on Facebook and feelings of sadness and loneliness. Not only that, but students who identified as "Facebook users," checking Facebook multiple times per day, had lower grade point averages and spent less time studying than students who did not use social networks.[52]

Another study highlighted in the same journal analyzed how comparing ourselves to others via social media can have a detrimental effect on our emotional wellbeing. In the study, participants were asked to keep a daily journal of their Facebook interactions for two weeks. The results showed a correlation between comparing themselves to others and feelings of guilt and sadness. This was even the case when participants perceived themselves to be better off than their friends/acquaintances.[92] As you can see, excessive exposure to social media can leave us feeling lonely, guilty, and sad about our current situation. To avoid experiencing these emotions in your life, consider reducing your daily social media interactions. Not only will the time you save from reducing exposure to these sites free you up to perform higher value activities, it will also ensure that you remain in a positive mental state throughout the day. If you're feeling really adventurous and are considering cutting off social media completely, you're not alone in your desire. Over the past few years, there have been many

Millennials who have made a similar pledge to walk away from social media. Many of them express how much this decision has positively impacted their lives. For a list of Millennials taking a social media hiatus, check out the awesome article provided below:

https://www.theguardian.com/media/2016/sep/21/does-quitting-social-media-make-you-happier-yes-say-young-people-doing-it

Reducing your TV time

Invented by a trio of brilliant scientists and first unveiled on January 26, 1926, the television was a revolutionary invention that changed the way communications were transmitted to the masses.[60] First marketed to the public in 1946, it didn't take long before the TV became the top source of entertainment for most Americans. Nowadays, televisions are mainstays in most American homes and are proudly displayed in the center of a family's living room. Although there's no doubt that the television is a technology that revolutionized the media industry, its effect on how we spend our free time is a cause for concern.

A Nielsen consumer report released in the first quarter of 2016 showed that the average American spends about five hours per day in front of the tube.[61] This translates to 35 hours per week! Considering the average American workweek is 40 hours, watching television has become most people's second jobs. How can you expect to get ahead in life if you spend the vast majority of your free time in front of the television? Not only is watching television a HUGE time suck, more and more studies show how detrimental watching TV excessively can be to our overall health and wellbeing.

In a new study published in the journal *JAMA Psychiatry*, researchers examined 3200 participants beginning at age 25 to see what effects excessive exposure to TV had on their cognitive ability over time. Every two to five years, the participants were put through a battery of cognitive tests to measure overall cognitive function.

After 25 years, the results showed that people who watched TV for three or more hours per day fared much worse than their counterparts in tests measuring cognitive performance. Not only that, but individuals who watched TV excessively were also more likely to engage in other detrimental activities such as making poor eating decisions and not exercising.[62] Now that you understand how bad watching television excessively can be for your overall health, what steps can you take to reduce your exposure over time?

I'm not saying you should cancel your cable, Netflix, Hulu, and other media accounts right away. Watching a series with friends and loved ones can be a relaxing and enjoyable experience. What I'm saying is that organizing your day around the next episode of your favorite show may not be the winning success strategy that gets you closer to achieving your BIG goals. Try reducing the time you spend in front of the TV by 50%. Although this may seem like a lot, the amount of time this frees up each week will allow you to pursue other worthwhile interests that can add value to your life. Use this extra time to connect with loved ones, practice a new skill, study a new subject, or read a good book. Over the course of a few months, I'm sure you'll notice the positive changes that come about as a result of your decision.

Developing your drive for success

"Success today requires the agility and drive to constantly rethink, reinvigorate, react, and reinvent." – Bill Gates

Have you ever been driving down a long stretch of road with no one in sight for miles? You grip the wheel tight, smash your foot on the gas pedal, and accelerate to a significant speed. The rush you experience is intoxicating, to say the least. The same intoxicating feeling is experienced when you accomplish a goal you've set for yourself. However, as with any goal you want to accomplish, you'll need to develop your drive for success to ensure that you battle through the tough times you'll inevitably face along the way. Having *"drive"* means pushing yourself to achieve your goals each and every day without fail. Although this may seem like a lot of work, if you take the time to outline a few important steps first, you'll be much more likely to stick with your commitment over time.

What's your "driving force"?

To start, it's important to determine what motivates you to get out of bed to tackle the day. Everyone has different reasons for wanting to accomplish success in life. However, you can allocate most desires into four separate categories. These categories are "WHAT," "WHY," "WHO," and "HOW." People who are driven by "WHAT" are driven by either an event in their life or the desire to attain something tangible. You often hear stories of people driven by "WHAT" mentioning how they wanted to achieve success to *"prove the doubters wrong."* Their haters' doubts and negativity helped push them to achieve the massive success they eventually attained. Along with that, people who are driven by "WHAT" may be motivated by material possessions. Someone who desperately wants a Lamborghini Gallardo may be willing to do whatever it takes to attain that car.

The second driving force of success is "WHY." If you're driven by a "WHY," it means you have an overall vision or creed you aspire to. People who are driven by "WHY" cultivate their desire by striving to accomplish this inner purpose each and every day. When they encounter obstacles, people driven by "WHY" reference their mission/vision to renew their motivation.

Many other people are driven by the external force of "WHO." If you're driven by "WHO," it means your drive to succeed is rooted in your desire to give and/or be the best for another person or persons. This inner desire pushes you to achieve great heights and overcome significant obstacles. Common examples of people who fit the "WHO" profile are kids, spouses, family members, and friends. These people offer inspiration to those driven by "WHO" to be the best they can be.

The final of the four driving forces is "HOW." People who are driven by "HOW" cultivate their desire to achieve success by taking pleasure in doing excellent work. They love the nuances and little details of each task and are excited when they execute their work to perfection. Those driven by "HOW" are willing to fight through obstacles because they have a relentless desire to execute each part of their role to perfection.

In my life, I'm driven by an inner "WHY" of wanting to help others achieve their goals through coaching and leadership development. All the free and paid content I produce is developed with this singular "WHY" in mind. My "WHY" gives me motivation to keep going even when I hit a writing slump, when I don't feel like waking up at 5:00 a.m. to develop new content, and when a new shiny distraction arises. I've provided the exercise that helped me define my "WHY" in the *Developing a Winning Psychology*" resource section.

Now that you understand each driving force, take some time to think about which one you most associate with. Although you may feel you're driven by more than one driving force, there's usually one main force that propels people forward. Write it out on a piece of paper and keep it somewhere where you can reference it easily. I personally hang mine on my bedroom wall so it's the first thing I see when I wake up in the morning and the last thing I see when I go to bed. This keeps my driving force front and center so that the next time I encounter an obstacle I'm able to reference it for motivation.

Following up with action

Although motivation is a big part of achieving success, it's not the only part of the equation. Coupling your "driving force" with action towards your goals is the true formula of success. However, what often happens is that people get extremely motivated to do something positive with their lives and then don't follow up with consistent action over time. As a result, they get discouraged and move on to something else. One of the most common examples of this cycle can be seen in gyms all across America. During the first few weeks of the year, there's an influx of new gym goers looking to stick to their new year's resolution of getting in shape. For those of us who are active gym goers, this causes some inconvenience because the gym gets extremely crowded. However, we know that the vast majority of the people who started their gym memberships in January will not be there come February. Why is that? Do they just not have what it takes?

The truth is that motivation can wain over time, especially when obstacles get in the way. If you don't resolve to push through these obstacles and perform the necessary actions each day, it's quite easy to fall back into your comfortable old ways. In a study published in the 2013 edition of *The Journal of Personality and Social Psychology*, researchers examined how students acted in high pressure environments when their willpower was depleted. It was shown that students who had a habit of eating an unhealthy meal before an exam were much more likely to engage in the same behavior on exam day. On the other hand, students who consistently ate a healthy breakfast tended to do the same on the day of the exam.[63] Why is it that students stuck to their default decisions even during stressful situations? It's because eating a healthy or unhealthy breakfast became a "habit." Even when their willpower was depleted, the students who ate a healthy breakfast were able to fall back on their default decision of eating a healthy breakfast. As we'll discuss in the *Developing positive habits* section of the book, deliberately performing an action over time will eventually culminate into a new habit. Your job is to identify that action and consistently execute it.

One of the ways I used this technique in my own life was by creating an action plan to write a minimum of 500 words each weekday for four months. Although there were days where I'd stare at my computer screen for an hour with writer's block, I'd eventually reach my 500-word goal. Sometimes my writing was so bad that I'd scrap almost all of it after my writing session. However, there were also days where I wrote 2000 words of solid content in one sitting. All it took was defining a metric and setting aside the time to make it happen. What actions can you take this week to move you closer to your goals? Write out three to five action items you'll consistently execute. Commit to completing each one before 5 p.m. every Friday. I know that if you actually stick to this resolution, you'll be well on your way to achieving the life of your dreams.

Valuing grit above all else

"True Grit is making a decision and standing by it, doing what must be done." – John Wayne

What do John D. Rockefeller, Henry Ford, Colonel Sanders, and JK Rowling all have in common? These extremely successful individuals all failed multiple times before achieving their ultimate success. John D. Rockefeller was a failing oil prospector before a close encounter with death changed the course of his life. Henry Ford's first venture failed, forcing him to declare bankruptcy. Colonel Sanders was a 62-year-old failed restaurateur before he started KFC, and JK Rowling was a depressed 30-year-old single mom living with her parents before penning the first draft of *Harry Potter and the Philosopher's Stone*. They weren't the smartest people around. In fact, there were many people who were much smarter than them. However, each and every one of these individuals had something the others didn't: grit.

We live in a society where talent is praised above all else. We look on in awe as we hear stories about prodigious musicians who learned to play the violin at age four or the coding geniuses who started the next big social media company. Although there are people out there who fit this bill, talent is not the only part of the success equation. In the book *Grit: The Power of Passion and Perseverance* by Angela Duckworth, Professor Duckworth explores how grit may be the key to unlocking your full potential. You may be asking, what is "grit"?

Grit is passion and perseverance towards a set of long-term goals. Grit is having stamina and approaching each challenge as a marathon, not a sprint. It's consistently sticking with one idea, one goal, or one objective for years. She contends that putting a substantial amount of effort into acquiring skills and then applying those skills towards achieving your goals are the formulas to achieving lasting success in any industry. Below I've provided each formula discussed in the book:

Talent x Effort = Skill

Skill x Effort = Achievement

When someone starts out learning anything, they need to dedicate the proper time and effort to acquire their desired skill. If the person is talented, they may be able to learn the skill faster than those who are less talented. However, since "effort" is accounted for twice when someone is looking to achieve something spectacular, it's actually a much more important variable for whether a person achieves the level of success they desire. By applying more effort into learning your craft and then applying more effort into applying that skill to achieve a goal, you can compound your results over time. My football coach would often say, *"Hard work beats talent when talent doesn't work hard,"* and he couldn't have been more right.

How to develop grit

Now that we've determined how important grit can be to achieving long-term success, let's delve into how you can develop more of it in your life. In the book, Angela goes over the parable of the bricklayer. In the story, three bricklayers are building a church together. When each bricklayer is asked about their role, the first bricklayer says, *"I'm laying bricks"* (a job); the second says, *"I'm building a church"* (a career); and the third says, *"I'm building the house of God"* (a calling). In this example, each bricklayer was performing the same action, but the third bricklayer viewed his role as extremely important and was driven by a higher calling.[58] A recent survey administered to a large British multinational company showed that workers who viewed their job as a calling missed on average one-third fewer days of work, were more engaged throughout the day, and on average put in 20% more hours of work per week.[64]

If the average person works 40 hours per week, this extra 20% translates to around 400 extra hours of work per year. That's almost three months of full-time work! If this effort is applied consistently over a decade, the individual who puts in 20% more hours will have amassed two more years of experience (4000 more hours) in the same timeframe. The moral of the story is that even if you don't currently view your work as a calling, try to figure out how your job lines up with your bigger purpose in life. The more passionate you are about the work you do every day, the faster you'll achieve mastery and fulfillment.

Developing a growth mindset

What would your response to the following question be: *"How do you view setbacks in your life?"* If your answer sounds something like *"I hate setbacks! They've never helped me achieve any of my goals,"* you may currently be suffering from a pessimistic mindset. In order to reach your full potential, you'll need to break away from pessimism and shift your mindset to be more growth focused. What do I mean by growth focused? I mean viewing negative stimuli in your life as an opportunity to grow and improve. For example, if you get passed over for a promotion, do you throw up your hands up and complain about how unfair the world is or do you objectively look at what you need to improve upon and then begin working towards that objective?

In a study conducted by Stanford University, elementary school students were taught how the brain responds to negative stimuli. When kids read about how the brain changes and grows in response to a challenge, they were much more likely to persevere when they failed because they didn't believe failure was a permanent state.[59] Have you been down on yourself because of a previous failure? Try to reframe your failure as a learning experience and envision how your brain is changing to respond to future negative stimuli. By viewing failure in this light, you'll be more willing to push through adversity when the going gets tough. Now that you've begun the process of developing more grit, you'll be better able to capitalize on the next part of the success formula.

Learning to play the long game

When I graduated from college, I was eager to make a big impact on the world. I started a pasta catering company in college and wanted to expand the business into other parts of Phoenix, Arizona. Also, I'd recently been accepted into a local business development program that taught entrepreneurs how to scale and operate a business. My plan was to open my first location a few months after graduation and five more the following year. Then I'd go nationwide and everyone in the US would enjoy my pasta dishes!

However, after a few months of prospecting and attending local networking events to solicit business, I realized that growing a catering company was a lot harder than I initially thought. This discouraged me, and I eventually diluted the business to pursue new opportunities. Now that I have more real-world experience I can see the error in my ways. Although starting a pasta catering company didn't align with my passion, I'm confident that I would have had more success in business had I learned to play the long game.

Earlier in the book, I explained how capitalizing on the power of the compound effect can help you achieve extraordinary results. If I'd been willing to preserve through the hardships and low points of the business development process, I would have achieved much better results. The first mistake I made was setting unrealistic timelines for my goals. I expected that I would open my first location only a few months after graduation. Although this was possible, I had never operated a restaurant and didn't have the proper experience to hire staff, keep the books, acquire the proper licensing, etc. Had I done the research beforehand, I could have created a focused plan to attack each obstacle as it came along.

Secondly, when I didn't hit my goal by my deadline, I was extremely discouraged and lost interest in pursuing the venture. This often happens with early stage entrepreneurs. We get so excited about our life-changing idea that we jump into it head first. However, when the first sign of trouble rears its ugly head, most of us run for the hills and/or lose interest all together. If I had taken the long approach, I would have been much more likely to attack each problem as it came along and kept my eyes on the overall goal.

Having learned from my previous mistakes, I now take the long approach with every goal I set for myself. As a result, I've written two books (and am mid-way through my third), I've presented to thousands of people across the US and abroad, I started a YouTube Channel and I ran my first marathon. I wouldn't have been able to accomplish any of these goals had I not approached each problem with the end goal in mind. Although it's important to play the long game when it comes to achieving your big hairy audacious goals, you shouldn't get complacent about putting in the effort required to achieve them. In the S.M.A.R.T. goal section of the book, we'll explain how you can structure your goals effectively to significantly increase your odds of achieving them.

Action Items

Developing a winning psychology

1) For the next 2 months, commit to writing out 3 positive experiences you had throughout the day. If after 2 months you notice a substantial improvement in your mood, continue the routine.
2) Write out your top 3-5 limiting beliefs. Commit to removing each one from your vocabulary.
3) Write out 3-5 positive phrases to replace your limiting beliefs with. Commit to reciting 1-2 each day for the next month.

Garbage in, garbage out

4) Commit to cutting your news consumption by 50% this month. Replace it with positive, uplifting content.
5) Cut your social media time by 50% this month. Use the extra time to connect with family, pick up a new hobby, read a good book etc.
6) Cut your television viewing time by 50% this month. Use the extra time to connect with family, pick up a new hobby, read a good book etc.

Developing your drive for success

7) Determine what your driving force is ("WHAT," "WHY," "WHO," "HOW"). Write it out on a piece of paper and hang it up where you can reference it regularly.
8) Each Monday for the next month, commit to writing out 2-3 specific weekly action items that will move you closer to your top goal of the year. Work towards each action item throughout the week.

<u>*Valuing grit above all else*</u>

9) Select a difficult topic you'd like to learn more about (e.g., coding, business writing, foreign languages, etc.) and commit to learning it over the course of the next 2 years. Every six months perform a check to see how you're progressing.
10) Think back to a time when you experienced failure. Remember all the positive things that occurred as a result of that experience. Reframe your perspective to view failure as an opportunity to grow.

For a printable PDF list of these action items, check out the link below:

https://bit.ly/2McuIXP

Chapter 3
Achieving happiness

◆

"Happiness doesn't depend on any external conditions, it is governed by our mental state." – Dale Carnegie

A question humans have been seeking to answer for millennia is the age-old question of, *"How can I achieve happiness?"* As one of the four major human emotions (fear, anger, sadness, happiness), it's no wonder we want to pursue the only positive emotion of the bunch.[37] There have been countless books written on the subject of finding happiness, but many fail to explain how the state of happiness truly works. In this section, we'll go over lessons we can learn from Buddha, how we can unlock our best self, and how to improve our mental framework to accept happiness into our lives.

Lessons from the Buddha

"There is no path to happiness, happiness is the path." – Buddha

On the eve of summer 2017, I used one of my Audible credits to purchase a book called *The Subtle Art of Not Giving a F*ck*. In the book, Mark Manson references the story of Buddha and how it helped him gain perspective into what true happiness is all about. The Buddha was born Siddhartha Gautama to a tribe leader in Northern Nepal in the sixth century BC. When Siddhartha was born, a holy man predicted that he would either become a great king/military leader or a great spiritual figure. Hearing this, his father sheltered Siddhartha from all the suffering of the world and isolated him in his own castle where servants catered to his every whim.

You would think that Siddhartha would be happy being in this situation, right? Well, as the story goes, he grew up with a feeling of emptiness and sadness. One day, he left the castle to explore the local city. There he saw an old man struggling to walk, a sick man on the verge of death, and a rotting body on the side of the road. These images horrified Siddhartha and he began to resent his father for keeping him sheltered from human suffering. He went down to the city several times after his initial expedition and on one occasion met a group of ascetics. Ascetics are people who practice extreme self-discipline and abstain from any form of indulgence usually for religious reasons. He became fascinated by their way of life and one day decided to leave his family behind to follow an ascetic life.

For years he starved himself, refused water, and experienced pain and suffering so that he could finally achieve enlightenment. However, when he didn't find it he felt lost and confused. He'd been suffering for so long and hoped that by doing so, he'd be able to achieve a higher state of being. One day after a young girl offered him a bowl of rice he realized that depriving himself of food, water, and basic necessities was not getting him closer to enlightenment. From that day on, Siddhartha encouraged people to follow a path of balance instead of one characterized by extremism. He called this path "The Middle Way."

That night, Siddhartha sat under a Bodhi tree (a fig tree) and promised himself he wouldn't get up until he achieved true enlightenment. Over the course of the next few days, Siddhartha meditated about life and the universe, and pondered the questions he had about suffering. In his meditative state, the picture of the universe became clear. It was in that moment he became the "Buddha" (he who is awake). The Buddha went on to teach his philosophies for the rest of his life, and today there are over 535 million people practicing Buddhism around the world.[27] I'm personally not a Buddhist, but Siddhartha's story and philosophies on life paint a unique picture of how a person can achieve happiness. Let's break down a few of the key concepts:

Understanding happiness is a state of being

As Siddhartha was living an ascetic lifestyle, he realized the secret to true happiness wasn't living in the extremes. When he was a young boy, he had been given everything and was pampered on a daily basis. Even though this was the case, he constantly felt empty and alone. His desire for something more in life compelled him to leave the palace walls and commit to the ascetic lifestyle. When he followed the ascetic lifestyle, no matter how much he deprived himself of basic necessities, he still didn't find the enlightenment he was in search of. Only when he adopted "The Middle Way" was he able to get into the right mental state to achieve enlightenment. What I interpret from this story is that living a fulfilling life is all about striving for balance. You need to experience the bad times to really have an appreciation for the good times. Not only that, you need to have good times in life so that when bad things inevitably happen you'll be hopeful that there are better times ahead.

Most people misconstrue happiness as an emotion that's achieved at a future date. *"I'll be happy when I get that promotion," "I'll be happy when I find that special someone," "I'll be happy when I have the body I've always wanted"* are just some of the phrases we tell ourselves to justify not being happy in the moment. What usually happens when we achieve a goal is that we may experience a "happy" emotion for a day or two. However, that emotion quickly subsides and then it's back to the grind. My question to you is, if you're constantly pushing off happiness until a future date, when will you ever truly be happy?

Having a desire to achieve a future goal is extremely beneficial, and I use my desire to propel me on a regular basis. However, what you must understand to achieve true happiness is that happiness is a state of being and not an emotion. True happiness is the work you perform each day to achieve your goals, it's your family and friends who support you, and it's your life with all its blemishes and bruises. Living in the present and having a genuine appreciation for your life is true happiness. One of the ways I've attempted to be more grateful in my life is to write out three things I'm grateful for each morning. This gets me in a proper state of mind to be happy in the moment and enjoy the day. Try this exercise out for yourself and see if it doesn't make you appreciate life a bit more.

Taking responsibility for your present state

Do you have a friend or family member who's always in a state of torment and anguish? Do they complain about everything and feel as though the universe is conspiring against them? Well, if your friend/family member was here with us right now, I'd tell them to get over themselves! The way you choose to view life has a lot to do with your overall happiness. Even when events take place that are truly life altering and terrible, there's always a silver lining that can be extracted from the situation.

For instance, let's imagine a scenario where you get a flat tire on the highway while speeding to a very important meeting. This would be an unfortunate scenario for anyone, and the negatives of the situation are staring you right in the face. You could get mad about the fact that your stupid tire decided to explode on the highway when you had somewhere very important to be. You could get frustrated at the mechanic who performed your last check-up because he/she should've made sure the tires were properly inflated. You could get mad at your cheap alarm clock for not going off on time, which caused you to speed to your appointment. Allowing these thoughts to invade your mind will probably put you in a negative mood for the rest of the day. However, what does getting angry at these external factors accomplish?

You can't control the fact that your tire decided to explode in the middle of the highway, you can't control what your mechanic did or didn't do during your last check-up, and you can't control the fact that your alarm clock didn't go off. The only thing you can control is how you decide to react. What would happen if instead of acting upset and pouty, you decided to approach your setback with grace and happiness? Think about how much better you'd feel throughout the day. Would you be able to tackle more difficult challenges in the future?

According to a study published in the *Journal of Positive Psychology*, simply focusing on "trying" to be happier could actually elevate your mood and improve your sense of wellbeing. In the study, participants were split into two groups and were given "happy" music to listen to. The first group was instructed to make a concerted effort to feel happier while the second group was instructed to not actively try to lift their mood. After the experiment, the participants were administered a survey asking different questions about their mood. Although both groups experienced a lift in mood, the first group experienced a much larger increase in mood than the control group.[29]

Making the effort to view your environment in a more positive light can have a significant impact on your overall mood and sense of wellbeing. If you apply this insight to the flat tire example, you could choose to value the extra time you have to call a friend or read a good book while you wait for AAA to show up. You could choose to be grateful that the situation was not worse than it was. Many people who get flat tires also crash and seriously injure themselves. This subtle mindset shift will leave you feeling happier, more grateful, and excited to continue your day. Next time you find yourself in a negative situation, take some time to pause and evaluate. Are you about to get angry over something you can't control? Are there other more positive responses you could give? My recommendation is to always choose to see the positive in every situation. No matter how dark and disheartening it may be, there will always be a silver lining.

Unlocking your best self

"There's only one corner of the universe you can be certain of improving, and that's your own self." – Aldous Huxley

As we go through life discovering ourselves, we'll inevitably find faults with many aspects of our lives. Whether we're too small, too fat, too boring, not funny enough, etc., we're all different and have distinct characteristics that make us unique and special. In this section, we'll explore techniques you can use to unlock your best self and continue to let your personality shine bright for others to enjoy.

Allowing yourself to be vulnerable

When I was in the seventh grade, I had a huge crush on this girl in my class; let's call her Meg. She was extremely beautiful and had long blonde hair and blue eyes. Every day I would talk with my friends about how beautiful Meg was and how I wished she'd be my girlfriend. One day a friend of mine decided to tell one of Meg's friends that I had a crush on her and asked if she felt the same way. Meg heard the news and told her friend to ask me if I'd be willing to ask her out. When the message was relayed to me, I jumped for joy. I couldn't believe Meg wanted me to ask her out! Although this was positive news, I was petrified. I'd never asked a girl out before, and even the thought made me sick to my stomach.

The next day, I remember sweating bullets. With each passing hour I kept second guessing myself and felt apprehensive about asking her out. At lunchtime I mustered up the courage to walk up to her group of friends. My palms were sweaty, knees were weak, mom's spaghetti, lol jk, but I was seriously nervous. I walked up to Meg, made eye contact, and blurted out, *"Hey Meg, want to go out sometime?"* The words hung in the air like puffs of smoke. I remember feeling so vulnerable waiting for her response. When it finally came, it rocked me to my core. She looked at her friends, then back at me, said, *"No thanks,"* and walked away. I couldn't believe it, what kind of sick girl tells someone to ask her out and then immediately rejects them?! I was crushed and felt as though I would never love again. Of course, I was 12 and everything at that age seems like the end of the world, but that experience taught me a lot about what it's like to feel vulnerable.

When I moved to the US at 14, I found that being vulnerable as a man was frowned upon. Even discussing your emotions with others would lead to discussions about how much of a "baby" you were—or some other expletive. I found it especially true when I started wrestling and playing football. Any outward display of vulnerability was considered a sign of weakness and was exploited by others. As a result of these experiences, throughout high school and even college I felt that opening up to others would lead to rejection and pain. I closed off many great people from seeing my true self and carried a façade for most of my college career. However, after meeting my current girlfriend, it all changed. With her I've allowed myself to open up and show her my true colors, warts and all. The best part of it is that she accepts me for who I am. She, like many others before her, could have criticized, complained, or straight up rejected me, but she didn't. The feeling of happiness and satisfaction her love brings me is immense, and I can't even begin to show appreciation to her.

When you allow yourself to feel vulnerable around others, you give yourself the opportunity to really get to know a person. If they're willing to reciprocate in their vulnerability, you'll find out so much about them that you never knew before. These are how strong and lasting bonds are built. Although the "Meg" scenario didn't play out the way I wanted it to, I still learned a valuable lesson from the experience. There will be times where you open up to people and they reject you wholeheartedly. This will no doubt hurt and bruise your ego a bit. However, when you find the right person and are willing to let them in, a whole new world of understanding and love is open to you. Commit to opening up more to the ones you love. Share intimate details about your feelings and special moments from your past. You may be surprised how eager and excited they'll be to reciprocate and love you for it.

Reframing social comparison

Have you ever watched a celebrity on TV and thought about how lucky they were? Have you doubted whether you could ever achieve their level of success? At the other end of the spectrum, have you ever seen a homeless person begging on the street and thought about how they could let themselves get into such a negative situation? If you answered yes to either of these questions, you're not alone. As social creatures, we're wired to constantly compare ourselves to others. This process of evaluation is referred to in academic circles as social comparison theory. The theory suggests that we compare ourselves to others with the hopes of defining where we fall on the social hierarchy of society. We use variables such as appearance, health, intelligence, ability, social status, wealth, or any other attribute to compare how we match up with others. Based on our perceptions of the person we're comparing ourselves to, we'll either make a downward comparison or an upward comparison. Each of these comparison types can have positive and negative effects on your self-esteem and overall happiness.[38]

In the example of the Hollywood celebrity on TV, most of us would make an upward comparison and focus on how attractive, successful, wealthy, and talented they are. The problem with this kind of comparison is that it often leads to us resolving that we can never achieve that level of success for ourselves. This fuels emotions of envy, low-self-esteem and taking pleasure in others misery (schadenfreude).[39] In order to counter these emotions, it's important to shift your perspective. Although it may be true that these celebrities possess many positive qualities, we often forget that they're also imperfect humans who experience joy, pain, suffering, and love like the rest of us. By shifting your perspective to view them in this light, you're better able to objectively look at what you can do to emulate their positive qualities and improve/eliminate any negative qualities. As a result, you'll be more likely to aspire to achieve their level of success for yourself instead of believing that it's unattainable.

In the example of the homeless person, most of us would make a downward comparison and focus on the negatives that got them into that situation. Maybe they're a drug addict and use all their money on drugs. Maybe they're an alcoholic who lost everything because of their addiction. Maybe they're just lazy and prefer to live off the charity of others. These thoughts may even have you feeling better about your current situation because you tell yourself *"at least I'm not living on the street."* However, notice how these comparisons are negative in their nature and don't elicit a sense of compassion or empathy.

What if they lost their job and are just down on their luck? What if they have an undiagnosed mental illness that keeps them from integrating into society? These scenarios are just as likely as the latter examples and are often overlooked when making a downward comparison. Research shows that by identifying with people who are less fortunate than us and recognizing our own vulnerability, we can increase the feelings of compassion and concern we have for others.[40] Try putting yourself in their shoes and think about how you would feel in their situation. By practicing this exercise in your day to day life, you'll be much more likely to offer a helping hand to those in need.

Comparing yourself to others is human nature and it's almost impossible to control. However, by reframing your upward and downward comparisons using the strategies discussed in this section, you can maximize the value you gain from these social experiences. In the *Achieving happiness* resources section of the book, I've provided a list of questions you can ask yourself whenever you're making a social comparison. Using these questions as your framework, you'll be better able to make beneficial social comparisons and gain value from the experience.

Laughter is the best medicine

Have you ever been around someone who's always smiling and laughing? How do they make you feel? One of my good friends from college fits this bill perfectly. He's always cracking jokes and is constantly in a great mood. I notice that whenever I'm around him, I laugh more, I'm more social, and I'm in a better mood as a result. There's just something about laughing and smiling that makes you feel great. In fact, the biology behind laughter may give us a better understanding of why that is.

In a report published in the December 2003 issue of the journal *Neuron* by a research team at Stanford, researchers examined the brain activity of 16 students as they watched various cartoons. Their findings showed that when the participants watched funny cartoons, various regions of the brain's limbic system, which is responsible for the regulation of dopamine, were activated. Dopamine is a feel-good hormone that helps regulate mood and motivation and supports learning.[47] Understanding the impact laughter has on your mood, how can we go about laughing more throughout the day? If you're like me, you may find it almost impossible to force a laugh out when it's unprovoked. You may also be thinking that you're no Kevin Hart and would have difficulty making others laugh. Well, according to a year 2000 study on laughter, you may not need to become the next big stand-up comedian to get yourself and others to laugh.

In various research studies conducted by Dr. Robert Provine, professor of psychology at the University of Maryland, Dr. Provine sought to discover how and why people laugh. Over the course of a few months, Dr. Provine examined over 1200 undergraduate students as they interacted with their classmates, friends, and loved ones. What he concluded, contrary to popular belief, is that people generally didn't laugh in response to a joke or pun. Questions such as, *"Where have you been?"* or *"It was nice meeting you too"*—hardly knee slappers—were far more likely to precede laughter than jokes. In fact, only about 10% to 20% of the incidents of laughter referenced in the study were a result of a joke or pun.

So, if jokes aren't the cause of laughter in most situations, what is? According to another study conducted by Dr. Provine, the answer may surprise you. When Dr. Provine asked various students to catalog their laugher experiences in a journal, he found that participants were 30 times more likely to laugh when they were surrounded by other people than when they were alone.[48] Merely surrounding themselves with friends and family increased their likelihood of laughing. What this means for you is that if you want to laugh more, you don't need to become the next Dave Chappelle or Louis C.K. You just need to hang out and expose yourself to more people. What a revelation! If you're currently having limited human interactions throughout the day, look for ways to increase your exposure to others in your community. One of the ways I engage with more people is by being part of various organizations. Many people join social organizations to meet people and engage with likeminded individuals. Therefore, joining these organizations can provide you with a great opportunity to get some laughs in throughout the week. In the *Achieving happiness* section of the book, I'll provide some other tips and recommendations you can use to laugh more throughout the week.

Learning the art of forgiveness

It's senior day at your university. You've planned out this day for months and are excited to share it with your loved ones. You give your boyfriend a call, but it goes straight to voicemail.

Everyone went out last night so you're not surprised it's taken him this long to get out of bed. You decide to stop by his place to pick him up before heading over to meet your friends on campus. However, when you arrive at his place you notice something strange. There's an unfamiliar car in the driveway and his roommate isn't home. You walk up to the front door and knock a few times. No answer. As a result, you open the backyard gate and go in through the back door. As you climb the stairs and make your way into your boyfriend's bedroom, you find him in bed with another woman!

You begin hurling insults at him and the girl as you storm out of his room. You get into your car and speed out of the driveway. Your heart feels like it's about to explode. As you pull up to a stop sign a few miles away, you pull over to avoid crashing into something and spend the next few minutes sobbing uncontrollably. How could your boyfriend have done this to you? How could he betray you like this?

In that moment you resolve to never forgive him and feel as though you'll hate him forever. Although this exact scenario may not have happened to you, I'm sure you've had people in your life betray you in some capacity. Whether it's a friend who insulted you behind your back or a boss who threw you under the bus in an important meeting, there are many situations in life where it can be easy to hate another person for their actions. These events often lead to resentment, distrust, and anger. Research even shows that if these negative emotions are harbored over a long period of time, they may negatively impact you in a host of other areas.

One such study examined various couples who were currently in or recently removed from self-proclaimed "good" or "bad" relationships. During the study, individuals who reported being in or just removed from "bad" relationships had higher levels of cortisol, a stress hormone, in their bloodstream. Not only that, but individuals in this group also experienced a spike in their cortisol levels whenever they talked about their significant other or ex.

Sustained elevated levels of cortisol in a person's bloodstream increase the likelihood of developing various degenerative diseases including diabetes and/or heart disease.[93]

Along with contributing to increased stress, another study has shown that harboring bad feelings towards others can lead to a decrease in a person's overall sense of wellbeing. In the study, 1500 participants were asked to recall situations in their life where they had forgiven someone and how inclined they would be to forgive others in the future. Participants in their later years (middle age and older) were much more likely to forgive others. It was also shown that individuals who referenced being more forgiving reported having a better overall sense of wellbeing than those in the less forgiving group.[94]

The problem with harboring negative emotions towards another person is that it gives control of your life over to that person. If you're constantly thinking about how much you hate someone, you'll never truly be able to move on from the negative experience. When you forgive the other person and let go of your negative feelings, you free yourself from your emotional shackles and take back control of your life. Below I've provided step by step instructions on how to start the process of forgiving others:

1) *Think about the event that hurt or angered you. Accept what happened and acknowledge how it made you feel.*

2) *Ask yourself what you've learned from the experience. How did it help you grow? By answering these questions you'll begin the process of reframing your negative experience into one of growth.*

3) *Envision the other person and understand that they're a flawed human being just like everyone else. No one's perfect and by acknowledging their flaws you'll be more willing to forgive them for their transgressions.*

4) *Finally decide whether or not you want to forgive them in person. This may be the most difficult of the four steps, but it can also be the most relieving. By forgiving the individual, you allow yourself to move on from the experience.*

Although you're forgiving the person for what they've done, it doesn't mean you condone how they handled the situation. The person still wronged you and you need to determine whether or not he/she is worth maintaining a relationship with in the future. In the book *The Book of Joy* by the Dalai Lama and Archbishop Desmond Tutu, the Dalai Lama explains how letting go of a relationship after forgiving someone may be the best course of action. Sometimes relationships cannot be healed and the best thing to do is to move on. However, by allowing yourself to forgive the person who has wronged you, you remove their control over your emotions and disposition. Has someone in your life betrayed you in the past? Are you still harboring negative emotions towards them? Try utilizing the four-step process listed above to begin the healing process and take back control of your life. Believe me when I say that your future self will thank you for it.

Loving yourself for who you are

I decided to write this section after a conversation I had with my girlfriend. Sensationalist media outlets have been damaging young people's perception of themselves by displaying unrealistic expectations of what true beauty is. They parade around tall/lean models and celebrities who have been made up and digitally modified to eliminate all signs of imperfections. These individuals are then held up as the TRUE standard of beauty and plastered all over in magazines, commercials, and other forms of advertising. Media and advertising in the United States is a 220-billion-dollar industry. Every day millions of Americans are bombarded with ads promising how this service or that product will make them feel better, look prettier, become smarter, and/or gain the love of others. These companies spend billions of dollars per year in an effort to capture your attention, play with your insecurities, and make you feel as though you NEED their product and/or service.

With all this money dedicated to capturing your attention and the new unattainable standard of beauty in place, it's no wonder so many of us have become insecure about the way we look and feel about ourselves. The question now becomes, how can we filter through the garbage and renew our sense of belief and love for ourselves? Well, studies have shown that the best place to start is with your core beliefs.

In a 1999 study published in the *Brazilian Journal of Psychology*, scientists sought to understand how changing core beliefs with trial-based cognitive therapy would affect the quality of life of patients suffering from social anxiety disorder. By the end of the study, participants who had undergone the trial-based cognitive therapy experienced improvements in general health, vitality, social functioning, and mental health. Not only that, but on a follow-up visit 12 months later, the results of the therapy were sustained![95]

To start, identify one limiting belief you'd like to eliminate and come up with a new positive belief with which to replace your old negative belief. Once you've settled on your new positive belief, gather 10 pieces of evidence to support it. Imagine that you'll need this evidence to strengthen your case in trial. Each day, recite your new positive belief in the mirror and offer evidence to support this new belief. Although it may feel odd, the first few times you do it, I promise you it works wonders. In the *Achieving happiness* resources section of the book, I've provided a worksheet you can use to identify and support your new belief.

Donating your time and giving back

Have you ever donated money or time to a cause you believe in? It made you feel pretty good, didn't it? A big part of our mission here on earth is to give back and support others in our community and around the world. Not only does giving back benefit others, but recent studies suggest it may even be good for our health. According to a 1999 study conducted by Doug Oman of the University of California Berkeley, elderly people who volunteered for two or more organizations were 44% less likely to die over a five-year period than were non-volunteers. This study controlled for their age, exercise habits, general health, and other negative health habits like smoking. Another study led by Stephanie Brown of the University of Michigan also showed similar results. She found that elderly couples who regularly helped their friends, neighbors, and family members, and offered emotional support to their spouses had a much lower risk of dying over a five-year period than those who didn't.[4] This lowered risk of death among "giving" elders can be attributed to reduced stress levels.

One of the ways I enjoy giving back is by mentoring engineering students and funding a scholarship to support university students who are passionate about business and engineering. Each month, I have a 30-60-minute conversation with each of my mentees to evaluate how they're progressing on their monthly, semester, and yearly goals. During our calls, we discuss things they need help with, what they can do to improve their performance in various areas of their lives and evaluate their monthly wins. I've found that my experience helping university students has been extremely fulfilling, and I look forward to continuing to do so in the future. What causes or charitable organizations do you support? Take some time to research and find one or two in your area that have missions that align with your values. Once you have your list, commit to donating your time and/or money to the organization. Your support and commitment will not only help others in your community but will benefit you as well.

Seeking to connect with others

Have you ever heard of *Maslow's Hierarchy of Human Needs*? It's a psychological theory proposed by Abraham Maslow in his seminal 1943 paper, *A Theory of Human Motivation*. Maslow's theory describes the five basic needs that humans seek to satisfy. These needs are physiological, safety, love/belonging, self-esteem and self-actualization. Since these needs are hierarchical, a person cannot seek to satisfy an advanced need without first satisfying a more basic one. For example, someone will probably not be too worried about connecting with others if they don't have food to eat or water to drink. Below I've provided a picture of the hierarchy:

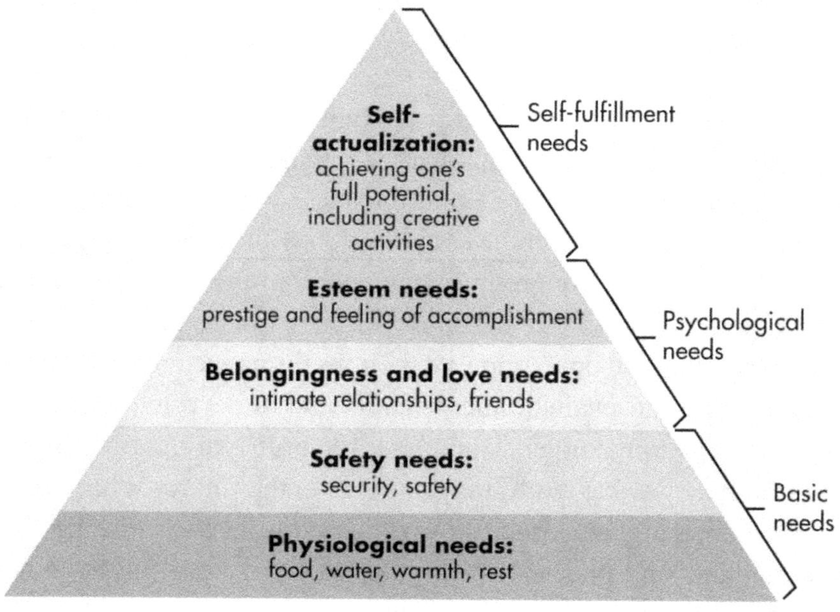

I've always found it fascinating that after finding food, water, and shelter, we need human connection to survive. This is why one of the worst punishments you can give someone is to isolate them from others in solitary confinement. We're wired to seek human interaction, and this wiring is one of the keys to achieving happiness in life.

According to sociologist Mark Granovetter, our social relationships can be broken out into two distinct categories, strong ties and weak ties. Strong ties are people in your life with whom you have a deep emotional connection. People in this category may include your parents, kids, spouse, significant other, close friends, etc. Weak ties are connections you only see on occasion. In a paper written by Gillian Sandstrom and Elizabeth Dunn published in the July 2014 issue of *Personality and Social Psychology Bulletin*, the professors conducted an experiment to figure out how strong and weak ties affected people's happiness and sense of belonging. In the experiment, 53 adults over the age of 25 were given two clickers. Over a six-day period, participants used the clickers to count the number of social interactions they had throughout the day. One clicker was used to count "strong-ties" and the other was used for counting "weak-ties." At the end of each day, the participants would rate their overall wellbeing and sense of belonging.

When the study was complete, the results showed that participants interacted with an average of 6.7 strong-ties and 11.4 weak-ties each day. Although the professors concluded that the *number* of connections each person had was not a good indicator of overall happiness, they did show that the *number* of interactions (especially with strong ties) was a strong indicator of happiness and sense of community. What this means for you is that if you want to become happier and have an improved sense of wellbeing, you should increase the number of interactions you have with your strong and weak ties throughout the day. Deepen existing relationships with your strong-ties by taking an interest in their lives. In the chapter titled, *Developing personal relationships*, we'll go over how you can build lasting relationships with the ones you love.

Determining your values

"Values are like fingerprints. Nobody's are the same, but you leave them all over everything you do." – Elvis Presley

As of early 2018, the world population stands at over 7.5 billion people. Although we're all human, we're all unique and possess our own particular set of values. When a person lives in line with their values, they achieve peace of mind knowing they're making decisions based on what they truly believe in. So, what are values? Your values are the things you feel are most important to the way you live and work. Think of your values as a compass you'll use to guide you on your life's journey. Throughout your life you'll refer to your values to determine which course of action to take. As a result, in order to live a happier and more fulfilling life, we must first outline what our most important values are.

To start, think of prior events in your life that made you the happiest. What were you doing? Examples may include spending time with family and friends, playing sports, working through a difficult math problem, etc. Once you've come up with a list of events, think back to the moments in your life where you felt the proudest. Why did you feel proud? Examples may include telling the truth even though it resulted in you getting into trouble, mentoring local elementary school kids, winning a high school or college sporting tournament, and/or receiving a big promotion at work. Finally, think back to the times you felt extremely fulfilled and satisfied. What need or desire did you meet in these instances? Examples may include completing a difficult work assignment that you were praised for, volunteering at a local charity, growing your small business, etc. Take some time to think about why these events were so memorable.

Now that you have your completed list of events that meet these criteria, come up with a new list of values that led to these outcomes. Examples of values may include accountability, courage, honesty, ambition, and many others. In the *Achieving happiness* resource section of the book, I've provided a list of some of the most common values held by individuals around the world. Use this list to garner inspiration and narrow down your list to your top five most important values. This may take a while, so allow yourself at least an hour to complete this exercise. Once you've identified your top five values, hang them up somewhere you can reference them regularly. These values will provide you with the clarity you'll need to answer some of life's most difficult questions:

1)   *What job should I pursue?*

2)   *Should I start a family?*

3)   *Should I start my own business?*

4)   *Should I compromise, or be firm with my position?*

5)   *Should I follow tradition, or travel down a new path?*

Congratulations for writing out your values! By doing so, you've started down a path of living life on your own terms. In the next section, we'll explain how defining what you're willing to suffer for can help clarify your overall mission and allow you to focus on what's most important in life.

What are you willing to suffer for?

You may be thinking that this is an odd question to ask. *"Why would I want to suffer? Couldn't we just avoid that altogether?"* As explained in the *Lessons from the Buddha* section, you'll inevitably face difficulty and suffering in life. The path towards anything worth attaining will require sacrifices that may result in pain and anguish. If you truly want a happy and fulfilling relationship, you'll have to learn how to deal with the arguments, disagreements, time commitments, and rejections that come along with nurturing a romantic relationship. If you want to grow a successful business you'll have to weather the constant rejections, the long work days, the fear of failure, and the self-doubt that comes along with operating a startup. The pain you're willing to endure will largely determine where you end up in life.

Is having a happy family life important to you? If you get more fulfillment from your family life than your career, you may decide to sacrifice the next promotion to be at home with your kids by 5:30 p.m. each day. This decision will come along with siblings fighting at the dinner table, discussions about poor grades at school, and kids crying about not getting their way. However, if this is something you're truly willing to suffer for, it will bring you happiness in the long run. On the other hand, if you choose to sacrifice having family dinners every night and are willing to suffer through advancing your career, you'll make the former decision. This decision will come along with long hours at the office, having to deal with difficult bosses, navigating company politics, and sacrificing time with your family and friends. However, if this decision lines up with your values and you're willing to suffer through it, it will lead to achieving happiness in the long run.

Whatever you decide, determining what you're willing to suffer for will simplify the decision-making process and propel you towards achieving your ultimate happiness. As we did in the *Determining your values* section, I'd like you to review your yearly goals and write out a list of three to five struggles you'll face on the road to achieving each one. If after writing out your list you feel that the struggles come with too big a price to pay, you may want to restructure your goal to line up with what you value in life. This is often a difficult exercise for my clients because it forces them to objectively look at their goals to determine if they're willing to pay the price to achieve them. Even if the answer to this question is "no," don't be discouraged. Just review your values and write out a new goal that lines up with these values. Trust me when I say, the extra time you spend on this process will save you a significant amount of heartache in the future. Now that you've defined what you're willing to suffer for, it's time to discuss how to get through the difficult moments in life when they inevitably arise.

Finding meaning in your suffering

We all feel pain at some point in our life. Pain can be either physical, mental, or spiritual and can have a substantial impact on our overall happiness and sense of wellbeing. One of the most difficult and painful events in a person's life is experiencing the death of a loved one. The loss of someone close to you can leave you feeling empty, sad, and unsure about the future. I experienced these exact feelings when my grandfather passed away in 2013. I spent most of my formative years in Europe and my Italian grandfather was one of my biggest role models. He was a no nonsense, old school Italian man who believed in discipline and the importance of hard work.

I would visit him every summer for two to three months at a time and they were some of the best times of my childhood. I idolized the man, and he loved my brother and me more than anything in the world. My grandfather was diagnosed with cancer in late 2012 and died shortly before I graduated from college (May 2013). When my mother told me the news, I was in denial about it. I couldn't believe that such a powerful figure in my life could be snuffed out in an instant. However, after a few hours of letting the news sink in, I broke down into tears. He didn't get to see me graduate, and that hurt more than anything. He always wanted me to get an education and have a better life than he had. He would've been so proud to see me walk across that stage. However, cancer had other plans and now I had to continue my life without him. For weeks after his death, I was in a state of grief and felt unmotivated to do anything. The one thing that helped me accept his death and move on with my life was finding meaning in my suffering.

In a study conducted by a team of researchers from the Department of Psychology at the University of Connecticut, the researchers analyzed 172 cancer patients to see if the way they perceived their circumstances affected their overall physiological wellbeing. The results of the study showed that participants who framed prior negative experiences as growth opportunities and found meaning in their suffering experienced a much more positive physiological adjustment.[43] Likewise, a recent scientific study found that individuals who went through the death of a family member and made sense of their loss experienced less distress than study participants who didn't find meaning.[44]

In Viktor Frankl's best-selling book, *Man's Search for Meaning*, Viktor shares his experiences during World War II as a Jewish prisoner in a Nazi concentration camp. The conditions Viktor found himself in were unimaginable. People all around him were being starved, overworked, and eventually gassed to death. How could anyone in that situation find meaning in all that suffering? One of the key observations he made during his time in the camp was that although we experience difficult times in life, we ultimately have the choice of how we respond to the stimuli. Two people can go through the same experience and, depending on how they perceive their situation, can have drastically different outcomes.[45] A tamer example of this response can be seen in supermarkets all across America.

Have you ever made a weekend trip to a Costco and seen the long lines that form? Have you observed how people react in these lines? Sometimes I look over and see a person's expression of anger and/or frustration as they complain about having to wait an extra five minutes line. In the same store I also see individuals who operate at the other end of the spectrum. Instead of getting upset about a situation they can't control, these individuals choose to be happy in the moment and use the extra time to enjoy the company of their family and/or friends. These individuals each experienced the same situation but had two completely different reactions.

If we apply the same logic to my prior experience, I could have taken the death of my grandfather as an excuse to be sad and grief-stricken and lose motivation for my goals. No one would have blamed me for it. In fact, many people would have wholeheartedly supported my decision. However, I could also choose to find meaning in his passing and use it as motivation to become the best person I could be. Although this road would be harder to go down initially, it would have the biggest pay off in the end. Once I realized I had the power to choose my response, I was able to use his death as a motivator to become a person I know he would be proud of. I'm not saying people should skip the grieving process entirely. Grieving is a natural part of the process of losing someone you love. What I'm saying is that as part of your grieving process, choose to find meaning in your suffering. You have the ultimate choice of how you respond to every event in your life.

Suffering is an inescapable part of life. In order to truly be happy in any situation, you must make a choice. Next time you find yourself in a situation that would normally illicit a negative response, objectively look at the situation and ask yourself, *"Do I have any control over what is currently happening?"* If the answer is "no," then choose a more positive response instead. By opting for this approach, you'll slowly begin developing a happier disposition.

You can't escape death

"It's not death that a man should fear, but he should fear never beginning to live." – Marcus Aurelius

The funny thing about time is that it stops for no one. The hourglass is always running and if you let the sands slip away, there's no getting them back. We often get too caught up with frivolous things in life. As a result, we live a life full of worry, stress, and eventually regret. Some of the best lessons we can learn about how to live our lives to the fullest are passed down from people in their golden years of life. For almost a decade Bronnie Ware, an Australian nurse and counselor, worked as a caregiver for the terminally ill (those who had less than 12 weeks to live). In her role, Bonnie provided counseling and therapy services to patients in an attempt to relieve their physical and mental stress. This kind of stress is natural when a human being comes face to face with their mortality. In her interactions with her patients, Bronnie asked them:

1) *Do you have any regrets in life?*

2) *Would you have done anything differently if life gave you a second chance?*

Over the course of a few years, she noticed that many of her patient's responses were similar. In 2012, she decided to write and share these lessons with others in her book titled *The Top Five Regrets of the Dying*. Below, I've outlined the top five regrets and analyzed each one:

"I wish I had pursued my dreams and aspirations and not the life others expected of me."

Many of her patients had been pressured by peers into a life they disliked because their loved ones, friends, and/or significant others expected them to conform to that reality. The pressure these individuals have on your life is unmistakable and extremely powerful. However, you should never let what others think influence what you decide to do with your life. In an interview with Amazon's founder Jeff Bezos, Jeff explains what made him decide to take a chance and start Amazon. Below I've provided his response:

"The framework I found, which made the decision incredibly easy, was what I called—which only a nerd would call—a 'regret

minimization framework.' So I wanted to project myself forward to age 80 and say, 'Okay, now I'm looking back on my life. I want to have minimized the number of regrets I have.' I knew that when I was 80 I was not going to regret having tried this. I was not going to regret trying to participate in this thing called the Internet that I thought was going to be a really big deal. I knew that if I failed I wouldn't regret that, but I knew the one thing I might regret is not ever having tried. I knew that that would haunt me every day, and so, when I thought about it that way it was an incredibly easy decision."

This is an extremely powerful way to approach life because you'll reduce the amount of regrets you experience at the end of your life. Do you want to quit your day job to pursue other passions? Do you want to expand your horizons outside of your current existence? Project yourself out to the age of 80 and ask yourself the same question Jeff Bezos did. Would you feel regret if you didn't take the chance? If so, take the leap of faith and live your life on your own terms. I promise you that your 80-year-old self will be glad you did.

"I wish I didn't work so hard."

In America, the idea of burning the midnight oil has become commonplace in our society. However, the demands on your time from work can put a strain on other areas of your life. Being driven to advance your career or grow your business is great, but not if you sacrifice all else in its pursuit. One of the areas most often neglected when fulfilling work obligations is maintaining healthy relationships with the ones we love.

One of the most famous cautionary tales about pursing work above all else is the story of Sam Walton. Although you may not know who he is, you've certainly heard of his company. With over 11,700 retail locations employing almost 2.3 million people, Walmart has become one of the most commercially successful companies in history. At the time of his death, Sam Walton had a net worth of almost 100 billion dollars and was listed as one of the richest men in the world. Although Sam had achieved a level of commercial success that few before him had, he died an unhappy man. Sam was known for consistently working 16-hour days and often neglecting his family as a result. On his death bed, his famous last words before passing were *"I blew it."* He realized too late in the game that chasing success without having anyone to share it with is not true success. It's OK to stop and smell the roses. You can have ambition in life while balancing it out by taking care of your personal relationships and health. If your current work environment is not conducive to living a happy and fulfilling life, consider shifting your focus and switching jobs. It may end up being one of the best decisions you ever make.

"I wish I had the courage to express my feelings and speak my mind."

To avoid rejection, many of us choose to follow the status quo. Although this may be the path of least resistance, there's a reason why it is. Speaking your mind and expressing your feelings is an important part of living a truly fulfilling life. If you're reluctant to express yourself to others, you may miss opportunities to change your life for the better. I wouldn't be with my current girlfriend had I not mustered up the courage to ask her out on our first date. Almost two years later, I believe it was one of the best decisions I've ever made.

I would've never had the idea to start my first blog had I not struck up a conversation with a random person on an airplane. During our conversation, we discussed the struggles he faced early in his career and the lessons he wished he would have known back then. This conversation got me thinking and I eventually started *The Strong Professional* blog to help other Millennials learn these lessons earlier in life so they could compound their results over time.

Don't be afraid to speak your mind and express your feelings. Some of the best opportunities you'll come across will require you to do so.

"I wish I had stayed in touch with friends."

Although we live in such an interconnected society, losing touch with friends is still a reality. Over time friends can grow apart and life moves on. It can be easy to go about your life without making a concerted effort to nurture relationships with old friends. While you shouldn't try to maintain relationships with ALL your old friends and acquaintances, it's important to engage with those special few. Start by setting up a text group and commit to FaceTiming each close friend at least once every few months. If you don't have an iPhone, I recommend using Skype. Skype is a software that allows you to make free video calls to anyone with an internet connection. I've provided a link to download the software program here (https://www.skype.com/en/get-skype/). Maintaining these healthy relationships will enrich your life and make it more fulfilling.

"I wish I had let myself be happier."

In such uncertain times, it can be easy to constantly stress about the future and focus on mistakes you've made in the past. This mindset of constant worrying, stressing, and being anxious is enough to make anyone's head spin. Learn to live life in the present and enjoy it for what it is, a long road with many twists, turns, and bumps along the way. One of my favorite lessons about living in the present comes from Zen Buddhist teachings. It states that there's no purpose in getting anywhere if, when you get there, all you do is think about getting to some other moment in the future. This constant worry and desire to reach a future destination will lead to unhappiness because you'll never be satisfied with what you have around you. Life exists in the present or nowhere at all. If you're unable to grasp that concept, you'll be in an unhappy state for most of your life.

To avoid experiencing this in your future, start by showing gratitude to people and positive events in your life. Did you just receive a big promotion? Celebrate and enjoy the moment. Did your significant other compliment you for completing some of the housework? Stop and show thanks for the comment. Did you look outside this afternoon and see a stunning sunset? Sit down and enjoy the view. Taking time to live in the present and being happy with your life is a skill that will serve you well in the future. Make a commitment to write down three things you're grateful for each day. I guarantee that if you continue this practice over the next few months, your mindset will shift and you'll feel happier and more fulfilled as a result. Congratulations on making it to the end of this chapter! By now I hope you've gained some valuable insight on how to live a happier and fulfilling life. In the next chapter we'll discuss how to develop and maintain healthy personal relationships with the ones you love.

Action Items

Lessons from the Buddha

1) Set aside time each morning to write out 3 things you're grateful for in life. This will teach you how to live in the present.
2) Take responsibility for your present state. If you don't like how you currently feel, commit to changing your mindset to a more positive one.
3) Allow yourself to be vulnerable around the ones you love. Set aside 15 minutes this week to address your feelings with your significant other, a family member, or a friend.

Unlocking your best self

4) Commit to opening up to someone you love. Set aside 15-30 minutes this week to have a conversation about how you feel about them.
5) This month, go to a funny movie, comedy show, or comical play with someone you love.
6) Think back to a time where someone wronged you and commit to forgiving that person for their transgressions. Perform the exercise highlighted in this section.
7) Donate 1-4 hours of your time each month to a charitable cause you believe in.

Determining your values

8) Use the information in this section to determine your top 5 values. Hang them up where you can see them.
9) Evaluate your yearly goals and determine what you're willing to suffer through to achieve each one. Write out a list of 2-3 challenges you'll face along the way.

10) Search for a charity that resonates with your values and set aside at least 1 hour every 2 weeks to give back in some capacity.

You can't escape death

11) Create a list of things in your life you want to accomplish but are fearful of. Make a commitment to move towards achieving one of those goals over the next 12 months.
12) Write out 3 things you're grateful for each morning.
    a. Once a quarter, reach out to a friend or family member and express how grateful you are to have them in your life.
13) Over the next few months, plan a vacation with your family, friends, and/or significant other.
14) If you aren't already pursing your dreams, create a 12-month plan with specific metrics focused on how you can transition to your new pursuits.

For a printable PDF list of these action items, check out the link below:

https://bit.ly/2MlXNiB

Chapter 4
Developing positive relationships

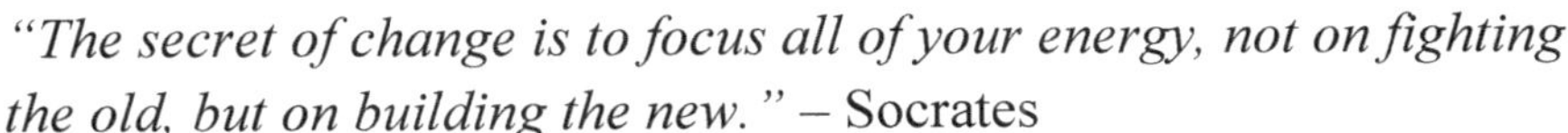

"The secret of change is to focus all of your energy, not on fighting the old, but on building the new." – Socrates

One of the most important parts of living a fulfilling life is maintaining strong personal relationships with your family, friends and significant others. Humans are social creatures, and we need to develop strong social bonds with others in order to survive. Although positive relationships can make our lives more meaningful and worthwhile, negative and draining relationships can have the opposite effect. How can you ensure that you maintain positive relationships while eliminating negative ones from your life? In this section we'll go over how to determine what relationships to let go of, what relationships to develop and grow, how to foster a healthy romantic relationship, and how to develop yourself so that you attract more positive relationships into your life.

Who do you associate with?

"People inspire you, or they drain you—pick them wisely." – Hans F. Hansen

Have you ever heard the expression, *"You are the average of the five people you spend the most time with?"* This phrase was popularized by Jim Rohn and describes how your associations have a significant impact on the success you ultimately attain in life. We humans are social creatures and have evolved to conform to societal norms. By surrounding yourself with negative influences, you'll naturally start to conform to their reality and lower your standards as a result.

Although this is not an exact science, there's quite a bit of scientific evidence showing the impact negative influences can have on your overall health, wealth, and prosperity. In a study conducted by Heather Walen and Margie Lachman of Brandeis University, the professors analyzed the effect different relationships had on a patient's stress levels. When a participant perceived a social relationship as negative, their stress hormones elevated to higher than normal levels.[15] Increased stress over a long period of time has been shown to lead to an array of diseases including heart disease, diabetes, and many others.

Not only that, but studies have shown that negative relationships can also negatively impact your actions. In a 2005 group study conducted by professors at the University of Minnesota, the professors sought to understand how associations affected overall health and wellbeing. The study was comprised of adolescent women from 31 different school districts in Minnesota with varying socioeconomic and racial backgrounds. Although there was significant diversity amongst the study participants, the results showed that influence from peer groups had a significant impact on whether the participant engaged in unhealthy weight control behaviors such as bulimia, extreme dieting, and/or over consuming diet pills.[16] Other studies have shown how negative associations related to alcohol and smoking can increase the likelihood of a person engaging in these activities.[17] Who do you regularly associate with? Are they people who lift you up or pull you down? Start by writing down the five people you spend the most time with. Once you have your list, analyze each one and determine whether they fall into one of these categories:

Disassociation

These are the negative influences you need to completely eliminate from your life. These people constantly complain, engage in detrimental activity, and consistently doubt your dreams and aspirations. Allowing people in the "Disassociation" group to take control of your life can lead to disaster. Leaving these people behind can be easier said than done, especially if they're family members. However, in order to reach your full potential, you'll need to distance yourself from these negative influences.

The Framingham heart study, which started in 1948, has regularly collected social and medical information from thousands of people living in Framingham, Massachusetts. Data compiled from this study suggests that emotions can be contagious. Each happy friend a person associated with increased their chances of personal happiness by 11%. However, sadness and negativity seem to be more infectious. For every sad individual a person associates with, their chances of being unhappy are doubled.[3]

Other research suggests that surrounding yourself with negative and toxic people can even affect your intelligence. Research from the Department of Biological and Clinical Psychology at Friedrich Schiller University found that exposure to negative emotional stimuli—the same kind of exposure you get by surrounding yourself with negative people and complainers—caused subjects' brains to have the same emotional reactions as experienced when stressed. Prolonged exposure to stress compromises the effectiveness of neurons in the hippocampus and can permanently damage neural pathways, inhibiting your ability to think clearly, reason effectively, and develop memories.[4]

Knowing all this, what steps can you take to reduce your exposure to toxic influences? If you identify an individual as a negative influence, have the difficult conversation with them to outline what your new priorities are. If they don't agree with your new life direction, it may be time to eliminate them from your life.

Although it will be difficult, it's essential for your long-term happiness and wellbeing. Just know that as you eliminate negative and toxic people from your life, you'll open the door for more positive and driven people to enter.

Limited association

These relationships consist of individuals you should associate with in a limited capacity. You may be able to have a great three-minute conversation with your neighbor, but he or she may not be a person you want to hang out with for three hours. On the other hand, you may have a high school friend who can be a great time for three hours, but you sure as hell don't want to spend three days with them. These relationships can be enriching and valuable if they're enjoyed in a limited capacity. Is there anyone on your list that fits this bill? If so, analyze how much time you spend with them on a weekly basis. Do you spend too much time with them? Once you determine what the appropriate amount of time to spend with each individual is, make sure to adjust your interactions with them accordingly.

Expanded association

This group is made up of individuals who bring positivity and prosperity into your life. They challenge you to be your very best and inspire you to grow as a person. These people are generally well-respected members of their communities and deliver significant value to those around them. You should always strive to surround yourself with people who fit this bill. Although they may not be easy to find, the value they can add to your life is immense. Look at your list and determine if you have any associations who fall into this category. If you don't know any of these people or you don't have enough of them on your list, make a commitment to actively search for them in your community. Attend events, conferences, and social clubs where these people regularly interact with each other.

Begin your search by researching groups such as Toastmasters, your local chamber of commerce, Lions Club, etc. People who fall into the "expanded association" category are always looking for ways to improve and as a result generally flock to these organizations. When you attend events hosted by these organizations, introduce yourself and converse with people. Are these individuals well-respected professionals in the community? Are they successful in various areas of their life (personally, financially, professionally, spiritually, family, health, etc.)? Would you want to trade places with them? If your answer to these questions is a resounding "yes," then you're in the right place to develop "expanded" relationships. Now that you've identified these individuals, form a relationship with them and look to add value to their lives. These kinds of associations often have demands on their time and may be unable to reciprocate in the relationship initially. However, the more value you bring to their lives, the more they'll be willing to offer advice and support when you ask for it. In the *Developing personal relationships* resources section of the book, we'll go over strategies you can use to develop relationships with these individuals. By utilizing these strategies, your list will soon be filled with only people who add extreme value to your life.

Periodically revise your list

As part of the process of shaping your list into one that contains more expanded associations, you'll want to revise it periodically to ensure you're on track to achieve your objective. Reviewing your list every few months not only helps you determine where you stand but also forces you to think of ways to improve your action plan. As Peter Drucker, the world-famous management guru, often said, *"What gets measured gets managed."* Measuring your progress as you develop more expanded relationships will ensure that you stay on track to reach your goal.

In a paper published in the journal of the *Institute for Quality Improvement*, Dr. Naomi Kuznets explains how revising her action plan during one of her projects led to significant improvement in the average wait times for a particular hospital. To start, her research group examined wait times across multiple hospitals, analyzed the operations of hospitals that were outperforming the competition, and developed an array of proposals for the hospital administration. Once everyone agreed upon the proper course of action, the researchers worked with the necessary parties to outline their responsibilities and organized a follow-up meeting to review their progress. When they came back three months later, they were surprised by what they saw. Although average wait times had improved, down to an average of 38 minutes, the hospital wasn't on track to hit their goal of reaching average wait times of 29 minutes by the end of the year. Over the next two weeks, the team reevaluated the plan and made necessary adjustments. As a result of their revised action plan, the hospital was able to reduce its average wait time to 29 minutes by the end of the year.[35]

What this means in the context of relationship building is that although you may have a solid plan to develop more expanded relationships, unless you measure your progress over time, you may be falling way short of your expectations. There will be times when toxic associations will try to creep back into your life and ruin your plan of replacing them with more positive influences. By setting aside time to review how you're progressing towards improving your associations, you'll be better able to tweak your plan accordingly. I set a reoccurring six-month alarm on my phone to review how I'm progressing in this area. By doing so, I'm able to ensure that the people in my life deserve to be there. Believe me when I say that taking the time to perform this exercise is worth more than you can imagine.

Nurturing romantic relationships

"A healthy relationship doesn't bring you down; it inspires you to be better." – Unknown

As Millennials, many of us are still learning a lot about ourselves and are searching for someone who can be our companion in life. No matter if you're straight, LGBTQ, or any other sexual orientation, having a companion to love and cherish is part of living a fulfilling life. How can we go about finding a person who will be our "Partner in Crime" and once we have that person, how can we show our love in a way that will support a happy and healthy relationship? In this section, we'll discuss how you can find the right person for you and go over techniques you can use to ensure that your significant other feels loved and fulfilled.

Understanding Millennial relationships

With the rise of social media and the impact it's had on our day to day lives, there have been quite a few misconceptions pegged to Millennials. We've been referenced by some media outlets as the "Tinder Generation" and are being defined as a generation of people who desire immediate gratification and have low value for commitment to another person. Although our generation is more free-spirited and open about our desires, we are no less likely than any other generation to seek companionship and love from another person. Although social media is a big part of our lives, it doesn't actually have as much of an impact on our dating lives as one might think.

In fact, many Millennials enjoy meeting people in ways other than social media. In a survey administered to almost 4000 Millennials, *USA Today* and www.Greatist.com asked an array of questions related to how the Millennial generation handles love and communication. One part of the survey showed that over 60% of Millennials preferred meeting new romantic partners through friends, groups, or shared interests. Only about 9% of those surveyed preferred meeting someone through a social app or website.[6] The rest of the survey participants still preferred meeting people at local meet-ups, get togethers, bars, etc.

Along with that, our generation is much less likely than previous generations to settle down and start a family right away. In a survey conducted by Pew Research Center, seven out of 10 Millennials (68%) have never been married, and the average age of marriage for our generation has climbed to 27 for women and 29 for men. When asked about the reasons for this shift, many Millennials referenced a lack of financial stability (29%), not finding the right person (26%), and their thought that they're too young to settle down (26%).[41] For many us, myself included, getting married and having kids is not a thought that's currently on our radar. Understanding how we as a generation perceive establishing romantic relationships is crucial to creating a plan of attack to find that special someone.

Outlining your perfect partner

Now that we've gone over how we as a generation think about relationships, let's delve into creating a plan of attack for finding a romantic partner. To start, begin by outlining what you look for in an ideal partner. Are they tall, small, or medium sized? What color are their hair and eyes? What features do they have? Although this may seem like a superficial exercise, performing it will give you an idea of what you find attractive in a mate. Now that you have a profile of the person you feel is your "ideal" mate, go over what personality traits you value most.

According to Ty Tashiro, PhD and author of *The Science of Living Happily Ever After: What Really Matters for the Quest in Enduring Love*, there are two basic ways to characterize someone's personality: horizontal qualities and vertical qualities. Horizontal qualities are external personality characteristics, such as masculinity, femininity, extraversion, and interests (music, sports, etc.). As Dr. Tashiro explains, *"...Matching on similar traits and characteristics doesn't predict long-term satisfaction and stability within a relationship."* For example, if you both love opera, that may be one argument avoided—but it's not a good indication of the relationship's success.

On the other hand, vertical qualities are made up of internal characteristics such as health, kindness, and overall disposition. Based on research, these characteristics are much better indicators of long-term relationship wellbeing.[42] What this means for you is that you should focus your personality list on characteristics that line up with positive vertical personality traits. Examples of these traits can be honesty, trustworthiness, kindness, emotional stability, positive attitude, etc. Take some time to write out five to ten vertical personality traits you most value. These traits will help complete your profile of your optimal mate.

Analyzing your profile

Congratulations! You've just come up with a profile of your optimal romantic partner. Although you should celebrate taking the first step towards finding your optimal partner, now comes the hard part. The question you need to ask yourself is, *"Do I embody the values I'm looking for in my optimal romantic partner?"* Are you honest, trustworthy, loving, hard-working, confident, and kind? Are you fit, healthy, driven, well respected, happy, and joyful? Go through your list and objectively analyze if you do in fact embody each characteristic. If you look at your profile and answer "no" to most of the traits outlined, you may need to evaluate what you can do to become the person who embodies those characteristics.

Now, I'm not saying you should focus on things you can't control. If you're 5'6", no amount of effort and hard work is going to get you taller than you already are. (Actually...I found these soles, and they seem pretty awesome: https://www.amazon.com/Height-Increase-3-Layer-Elevator-Inserts/dp/B072Q9XBJB/ref=cm_cr_arp_d_product_sims?ie=UTF8.) What I'm saying is that there are things within your control you can improve upon to make yourself more attractive to your optimal romantic partner. If you're someone with low self-confidence, start attending public speaking organization meetings, such as Toastmasters, to become a better public speaker. This may terrify you initially, but the skills and values you gain from the organization will increase your confidence and help you interact better in a social setting. Are you overweight and unhealthy? Try modifying your eating habits to eat a healthier diet. Prep your meals for the week ahead of time and commit to performing a 30-minute exercise routine three to four times a week. Are you always breaking your promises to others? Commit to keeping all your promises for the next three months. If you break a promise during that timeframe, donate $100 to charity. Over time, you'll begin cultivating a character trait of honesty and will attract others who share that same trait.

The power of visualization

Have you ever imagined something long and hard enough that it eventually came true? Maybe you wanted to win a sports championship, buy a new house, or play the piano in front of a packed house. Well, studies show that the act of visualization can actually get you closer to achieving your goals. In the early '90s, Alvaro Pascual-Leone, Professor of Neurology at Harvard Medical School, conducted a number of experiments with the hopes of discovering how the brain learns new skills. In one of his most famous studies, two groups of piano novices, individuals who had never studied piano before, were tasked with playing a sequence of notes on the piano. The professor taught each group how to play the sequence and instructed them on how to move each finger to play the notes.

After their initial interaction, the professor challenged each group with practicing two hours a day for five days. The difference was that group #1 was instructed to physically practice playing the notes on the piano while group #2 was instructed to imagine themselves playing the notes. After five days, each group was tested on their ability to play the musical sequence. Miraculously, although group #2 never actually played the piano after their first practice session, they performed just as well throughout the five days as the group who physically practiced the song![43] When asked about the results of the study, Professor Alvaro described it this way: *"...Mental simulation of movement activates some of the same central neural structures required for the performance of actual movements."* The activation of these neural pathways allowed participants who didn't physically perform the action to acquire the knowledge of how to play the notes on the piano.

What this means for you is that by visualizing your optimal match and envisioning what it's like to be with them, you'll put yourself in a better position to attract them when they do come along. Although visualizing your match can be helpful, unless it's followed up with action towards attaining your desired relationship, you'll find it extremely difficult to find that special someone. As an example, success coach Darren Hardy often describes how he used the power of visualization and self-reflection to find his beautiful wife, Georgia. He started by writing out exactly what he wanted in a romantic partner. He described the color of her hair, her family, how many siblings she had, her features, her character traits, her sense of humor, etc. Once he was done with his list, he looked inward and asked himself if he was a person a woman like that would be attracted to. From there he set out to become the best version of himself and visualized his perfect partner every single day. He began frequenting establishments where he could find that caliber of women, and he eventually met his lovely wife Georgia. When Darren describes meeting her he often says, *"It was as if she was the living embodiment of the person I had described in my notebook earlier that year.* " Although I don't necessarily think you need to write as much as he did—he wrote more than 40 pages describing his perfect match—it just goes to show how powerful visualizing and acting upon your desires can be. Try this visualization exercise for yourself and see what a difference it makes.

Learning how to treat your significant other

Congratulations! You've either found or are currently in a positive romantic relationship. Although you may be excited about the prospect of growing your relationship in the future, it can be hard to appropriately express your feelings towards your partner. This is especially true when other commitments, such as work, family, friends, hobbies, etc., start vying for your attention. In this next section we'll go over a scenario of a driven Millennial couple looking to excel in their roles at work while maintaining a healthy and prosperous relationship at home. What steps can this couple take to balance out their external commitments while fostering a growing and loving relationship? Let's jump in and find out:

Ben and Mary are a Millennial couple living and working in Seattle, Washington. Mary is a nurse at a local hospital and Ben is an engineer at Microsoft. Both Ben and Mary are driven people whose jobs are very demanding. Mary often works nights and weekends while Ben doesn't usually get home until after 7:30 p.m. most weekdays. As a result of their conflicting schedules, their love life has begun to suffer. Mary feels as though Ben doesn't spend enough quality time with her, and Ben feels that Mary doesn't appreciate the sacrifices he's made to maintain their standard of living in Seattle. This is a common scenario that plays out for many driven Millennial couples.

External demands can eat away at our attention and we may feel as though we don't have enough time in the day to dedicate to nurturing our relationship. In the book, *The 5 Love Languages* by Dr. Gary Chapman, Dr. Chapman examines the five love languages people commonly use to express and receive love. Humans need loving relationships to live a happy and healthy life. If you can identify your partner's primary love language, you can begin expressing your love in a way that will nurture a healthy and long-lasting relationship over time.

Words of affirmation

In the book, Dr. Chapman identifies "words of affirmation" as the first of the five love languages. Words of affirmation include words that encourage, support, and express love towards your partner. Examples of affirmative phrases include *"You're doing an awesome job babe!", "Whatever you decide, know that I'll be there for you."* and *"I believe in you and I know you can do it!"* etc. People whose primary love language is words of affirmation will take these words as signs of your love and affection.

In the case of Ben and Mary, Ben's primary love language is probably words of affirmation. He's been feeling neglected because Mary hasn't expressed gratitude for all the hard work he's done over the course of the year. If Mary wanted to make Ben feel loved, she could express her appreciation for all his hard work and thank him for the sacrifices he's made to maintain their lifestyle. These affirmative phrases will make Ben feel appreciated, and he'll be more willing to reciprocate love back to Mary.

Quality time

The second love language is that of "quality time." Individuals whose primary love language is quality time value one-on-one focused interactions with their partner. Now, just hanging out in the same room as your partner doesn't mean you're spending quality time with them. Coming home and sitting in front of the TV as your significant other tries to talk to you is not a quality interaction.

Activities such as taking a walk with your partner, getting away for a weekend together, and going out on the town for a nice dinner are examples of quality interactions.

In the case of Ben and Mary, Mary's primary love language is probably quality time. If Ben wanted to make Mary feel loved, he could take her out to a nice restaurant for a romantic dinner. This will help them reconnect as a couple and will have Mary feeling over the moon.

Gift giving

The third love language is that of "gift giving." Gift giving is part of the courting process for many different cultures around the world. People whose primary love language is gift giving feel love when they receive gifts or trinkets from their significant other. This can be as simple as a flower you find in the park or as extravagant as a tropical vacation to a beautiful destination. Although you may be thinking this love language could get expensive, not all gifts have to cost money. In the book, Dr. Chapman gives examples of gifts that cost no money at all.

Some of these gifts include an exotic feather you found in the park, a smooth stone you found on your stroll, a handmade card telling your significant other how much you love them, or a piece of finished wood with your names carved into it. Oftentimes, these gifts are more appreciated by your significant other because of their sentimental value. If your significant other's love language is gift giving, try hand making a card to express your love and appreciation. I have a feeling they'll be glad you did.

Acts of service

The fourth love language described in the book is "acts of service." This love language is expressed via acts of service for another individual. These acts include chores such as cooking, cleaning, laundry, taking out the trash, as well as helping your significant other with things important to them. Activities such as preparing for a work presentation or helping them work on their favorite hobby are also examples of acts of service. Nowadays this love language creates quite a bit of controversy because it can be misinterpreted as a way to perpetuate gender roles.

However, if your partner's primary love language is acts of service, nothing will speak louder than making her/him dinner one night a week or offering feedback on their work presentation. Make the commitment to do something in service to your partner this week and see what a positive difference it makes in your relationship.

Physical touch

The final love language is that of "physical touch." This love language is characterized by physically touching your partner and showing affection. For individuals whose primary language is physical touch, there's nothing better than cuddling in the morning or holding hands while watching a movie. Although this may seem like a relatively easy love language to satisfy, many people have a hard time expressing their love in this way.

This is especially true for individuals who didn't grow up in a family that was physically affectionate. If this is the case for you, I suggest trying to make expressing love in this way a priority. It may feel uncomfortable at first, but the satisfaction you'll bring your partner will be well worth it.

Applying these methods to your relationship

After a heated argument one night, Ben and Mary knew they had to change how they approached their relationship. They picked up a copy of the book, *The 5 Love Languages,* and began the process of identifying each other's love language. After much deliberation, Ben concluded that Mary's love language was "quality time," and Mary determined that Ben's language was "words of affirmation." With this new information in hand, they began to craft their plan of attack to best satisfy each other's needs. Ben began taking Mary out to a new restaurant once a week where they could enjoy a nice meal together while Mary began expressing appreciation for all the hard work Ben had been doing to maintain their standard of living.

After a few months of this routine, Ben and Mary's relationship is better than ever, and they're excited for their future together. Now that you understand each love language, go out and try to identify what your partner's love language is. A quick way to identify their primary love language is to see how your significant other expresses their affection and what they most complain about. These data points will give you potential clues you can use to identify their love language.

Improving your existing relationships

"It's futile to put personality ahead of character, to try to improve relationships with others before improving ourselves." – Stephen Covey

Throughout this section, I've stressed the importance of finding the right people to include in your inner circle and how to find the right partner for you. Now that we have those pieces in place, it's time to go over how to make your existing and future relationships as great as they can be. Since we know we can't control others and that trying to do so only leads to misery, the success of these relationships starts and ends with you. What can you do to improve yourself so that your important relationships flourish and improve your life for the better? In this section, we'll go over some strategies you can implement to do just that:

You get what you tolerate

Do you have a friend who's perpetually late to everything? They constantly hold up the group and show up to events well after they're expected to. Why do you think that's the case? Are you in a relationship where your significant other is deceitful and regularly cheats on you? Although I don't condone any adulterous behavior or deceit in relationships, why do you think they conduct themselves in that way? The answer to these questions may shock you. The reason is because it's TOLERATED.

Every time your group of friends waits for that friend, your friend is validated in knowing that even if he/she is late, your friends will wait around for them. Every time you kiss and make up with your significant other after they've lied and cheated on you, you've validated their belief that they can make things better after they've done those horrible things. These are the kinds of enabling actions that perpetuate bad behavior. Success coach Darren Hardy put it best when he said:

"You get in life what you tolerate. If you tolerate being disrespected, you will be disrespected. If you tolerate people showing up late and making you wait, people will forever show up late for you. If you tolerate being under-paid and overworked, that will continue for you. If you tolerate your body being overweight, tired, and perpetually sick, it will be. It's amazing how life will organize around the standards you set for yourself."

If you want to have more respectful and loving relationships, you must first expect others to handle themselves in the appropriate manner. When someone goes against what you're willing to tolerate from the relationship, you should immediately denounce that behavior. For example, the next time your friend runs late, continue along with your night as planned. Make him/her catch up with the group once they're ready. They may complain about the inconvenience for a while, but eventually they'll conform to the behavior that's expected of them. If your boyfriend or girlfriend cheats on you, eliminate them from your life. You'll no longer tolerate people treating you with disrespect and know that there are many others out there who are eager to treat you right.

What are some of the negative behaviors you've been tolerating in your life? Write a list of three to five negative behaviors and specify the people in your life who are exhibiting these behaviors. Once you have your list, make a commitment to not tolerate these behaviors going forward. Although it may be difficult at first, as you persist you'll begin to see how people adapt to your new way of viewing the world.

Don't drink your own Kool-Aid

Have you ever seen the old Kool-Aid commercials? In the commercial, a giant talking jug of Kool-Aid bursts into an unsuspecting family's home, chants its famous catchphrase, *"Oh yeah!"* and leaves the family's wall destroyed. In my life, I've met many people who are similar to the Kool-Aid man in that they want to make their presence felt and want you to know how great they are. This personality trait is often referred to as narcissism. Narcissism is categorized by an over inflated ego and desire for attention and recognition. Not only is this behavior rather annoying, it may be driving people away from you altogether. In a study conducted by Johanna Lamkin of Baylor's School of Medicine, 54 undergraduate student couples were asked how they would plan a hypothetical five-day vacation with a $3,000 budget. Their 10-minute responses were videotaped and evaluated by trained personality experts, who evaluated three traits:

1) Positive effect: How much they seemed to enjoy the task.

2) Anger: Signs of fighting (confrontational style, raised voices); angry tone of voice (frustration, annoyance); and subtler passive displays of anger, such as pouting or turning away.

3) Hostility: Rejecting or hurtful comments *("you're stupid," "you're a lousy travel companion")*.

Although some participants who exhibited narcissism did engage in affectionate behavior, on average participants who engaged with narcissistic partners were much more likely to experience anger and hostility. If these negative emotions are compounded over time, they can lead to resentment and eventual separation from your partner.[96]

Not only does having a superiority complex cause conflict within relationships, there are many past examples of people with large egos who have fallen from grace and lost it all. One such example was portrayed in the book *Ego is the Enemy* by Ryan Holiday. In the book, Ryan references the story of George St. Pierre (GSP). GSP was a three-time UFC welterweight champion of the world and is often referred to as one of the greatest UFC fighters of all time. When he beat Matt Hughes to win his first welterweight championship, he admitted to feeling invincible. He remembers being extremely cocky and believing that no one in the world could beat him. However, in a title defense against little-known fighter Matt Sera, he was knocked out in the first 90 seconds of the fight. GSP was an 11-1 favorite, and Sera's win is still considered one of the biggest upsets in UFC history. Luckily, after a period of self-reflection, GSP realized that his ego had gotten the best of him. From that day on he committed to never let his ego get in the way again. As a result of his renewed commitment to the sport, he eventually won back his title and didn't relinquish it until his retirement.[108]

Acknowledging his ego and taking steps towards resolving this problem is one of the main reasons GSP was able to eventually win back the belt. Is your ego similar to that of GSP's prior to his fight with Matt Sera? Do you think you're invincible and can do no wrong? Do yourself a favor and focus on toning down your ego a bit. Everyone has something they can improve upon and taking some time to figure out what those things are will pay huge dividends in the future. Over the next week, ask yourself a few of the following questions:

1) *Do I ask for transparent feedback?*

     a. *Do I get upset when it's given to me?*

2) *What areas of my life can I improve upon?*

3) *What are some of my shortcomings?*

4) *What can I do today to improve my wellbeing tomorrow?*

By objectively reviewing your situation and bringing yourself back down to earth, you'll develop a healthier ego and attract more love and happiness into your life.

Becoming a better listener

We all know someone who loves to talk about themselves. I've found that conversations with these people aren't really conversations at all. They're just 30-minute commercials about their life and problems. I try to avoid interacting with these individuals whenever possible because they add little value to my day and my life. Although you may not be as bad as the above-mentioned persons, most of us think we're better listeners than we actually are. In fact, in a recent survey administered by Wright State University, over 8000 respondents rated themselves on how effectively they listened when compared to their peers. The surprising results showed that almost everyone rated themselves "just as effective" or "more effective" listeners than their peers.[65] How is it possible that almost everyone in the survey thought they were an above average listener when on average, people listen with about a 25% efficiency[66]? Lucky for us, science may have an answer.

In a joint study into appearance conducted by psychologists at the universities of Chicago and Virginia, participants were shown digitally modified images of themselves, some of which were altered to make them look more attractive while others were altered to make them look less attractive. When the participants were asked to identify the unaltered images, they tended to select the enhanced version of themselves. However, when shown images of others in the group, participants correctly identified the unaltered images.[67]

We as humans tend to paint a rosier picture of ourselves than is actually the case. The reason for this seems to be hardwired into our brains. Since we evolved to operate in a social world, our ability to physically survive (and thrive) is in many ways tied to our ability to operate in a social context. Therefore, it's thought that, *"...The ego can be viewed as a tool that evolved to improve the odds of individual survival in the world."*[69] Given this information, it's no wonder we perceive ourselves as better than we are. Our very survival depended on it!

However, if we want to become better listeners, we have to put our egos aside and reflect on ways we can improve. One of the best ways to become a better listener and increase your likability is to ask follow-up questions. In a meta-analysis conducted by a team of researchers at Harvard University, researchers dissected the findings of various studies to better understand what characteristics make people more likable. What they found was that individuals who asked more follow-up questions were perceived as more likable. As stated by lead researcher Karen Huang, *"...Verbal behaviors that focus on the other person, such as mirroring the other person's mannerisms, affirming the other's statements, or coaxing information from the other person, have been shown to increase liking."*[109]

Commit to talking less in most interactions and learn to ask follow-up questions. In the context of building a positive relationship, learn to approach others with interest and a genuine desire to learn more about them. People love talking about themselves, so once you get the ball rolling, they'll be more than willing to engage in conversation. Be humble, stay focused, and be willing to admit when you're wrong. If you commit to nurturing these personal traits, you'll be well on your way to building healthy relationships with others.

Learning to say no

What word is so simple that it requires only two letters to spell, yet is so powerful that it elicits an immediate response? If you read the title of this chapter, you probably figured out that this word is "No." In the context of relationship building, the reason why no is such a powerful word is because it's a finite phrase that usually eliminates a person's commitment from having to perform a particular task. I learned the value of saying no during my junior year in college. At the time, I was involved in various student organizations and had an extremely demanding college workload that kept me busy.

However, I'd often find myself accepting new challenges/commitments because I either didn't want to let someone down or I had a genuine interest in the new project. On top of that, I had a jam-packed social schedule and constantly accepted invitations from friends to hang out. Although many people may envy my situation, all these commitments only increased my stress levels and made it difficult for me to enjoy my interactions with friends when I was around them. As a result, I always felt extremely anxious, and I wasn't able to perform any of my commitments effectively. All that changed when I decided to re-prioritize my commitments and only focus on the ones that lined up with my values and goals. I decided to drop out of one of my student organizations so I could focus more on my side business venture. I also declined certain invitations from friends so that I could commit to nurturing the relationships that were the most important to me. By reducing my overall commitments, my stress levels decreased, my overall happiness increased, and I finally felt as though I was back in control of my life.

Although you may now see the value of learning to say no, you may still be wondering, *"If I say no to some things, won't I miss out on the benefits of these opportunities?"* The answer to this question is a resounding YES, and that's the point! I'm not suggesting that you go out and say no to every opportunity that comes your way. Don't become Jim Carrey from the beginning of the movie *Yes Man*. What I'm saying is that, in order to have the time and energy to focus on the things you truly care about, you'll have to say no to some opportunities. You can't be everything to everyone. Following this path will lead down a road of stress, worry, and perpetual unhappiness. My suggestion is that if you let go of FOMO, fear of missing out, you'll be able to focus your efforts on the things in your life that do matter. This could be spending more time with your family and friends, exercising at the gym, working on that passion project of yours, etc. Saying no to propositions that don't line up with your values and goals is not only your obligation, it's a pre-requisite for living a happy and fulfilling life.

However, this can be a very uncomfortable thing to do because it elicits a confrontational interaction with the person you're saying no to. This is especially true when we already have a jam-packed schedule. The counter-intuitive results of a study highlighted in the book *Scarcity: Why Having Too Little Means So Much* by Harvard behavioral scientist Sendhil Mullainathan and Princeton economist Eldar Shafir sheds some light on this topic. Their research showed that as we get busier and our schedules fill up, we're actually MORE likely to say yes to new opportunities![34] This is because the busier you get and the more commitments you take on, the more depleted your willpower will be upon your next request.

In order to combat this phenomenon, try practicing your reason for saying no ahead of time. An example of an effective response would be, *"I wish I could, but I can't take on any more responsibilities this week."* This response diffuses the situation because you express your interest in the activity but are also firm enough so that the person you're responding to knows that you have other responsibilities on your plate. Try crafting and practicing your response at home. Step in front of the mirror and practice saying it with compassion and grace. Believe me when I say people will respect you for it.

Making time to nurture relationships

With all the information we've gone over in this chapter, you may be wondering, *"How am I ever going to be able to apply all these strategies into my life? I'm just too busy."* The famous writer Charles Buxton often said, *"You'll never find time for anything. If you want the time you must make it."* In order to ensure you spend quality time with the people you've deemed important in your life, you'll have to schedule it in your calendar. Success coach Darren Hardy takes this approach to the extreme. As part of his plan to maintain connections with those most important to him, he employs the 3-15-5-1 strategy. As part of this strategy, each week Darren makes sure to have three in-person meetings (breakfast, lunch, a long walk, etc.); send 15 written communications (texts, email, handwritten notes, etc.); make five phone calls; and give one small unexpected gift. To make sure he meets his commitments, he uses his journal to log all of these interactions.

I'm not saying you should do anywhere near the amount of work he does to maintain relationships. After all, many of these are key business relationships that will help his business grow over time. What I'm saying is that if Darren Hardy, an extremely successful coach and entrepreneur, can find the time to stick to this strategy, you can set aside a little time each week to dedicate to nurturing your most important relationships. Each commitment doesn't have to be extremely time consuming either. It can be as simple as scheduling a 15-minute call with a friend you haven't spoken to for a while or FaceTiming your parents for 15 minutes to see how they're doing. Over the next month, commit do setting aside time in your schedule to engage with the ones you love. Whether that's planning a three-day vacation with your college friends, buying a plane ticket to go home for Thanksgiving, or setting up a Friday date night with your significant other, setting aside time in your calendar to perform these actions will pay dividends in the future.

Action Items

Who do you associate with?

1) Write out a list of the top 5 people you spend the most time with.
    a. Analyze each person and place them into one of the "buckets" discussed in this section.
    b. If a person is not meeting your new high standards, start reducing the time you spend with them.
2) Make a list of 3-5 places where you can meet more "expanded" associations.
    a. Make a commitment to attend at least 2-3 events hosted at these locations.
3) Set an alarm on your phone to analyze your associations list every 6 months.

Nurturing romantic relationships

4) Set aside time this week to outline your optimal romantic partner. Be descriptive.
5) Objectively look at your list and determine if you embody these qualities yourself. If not, create an action plan to work towards adopting these qualities in your own life.
6) Perform a visualization exercise each morning where you envision being with your optimal romantic partner.
7) This week, sit down with your significant other and determine what their love language is. Once you define their love language, commit to expressing your love in that way going forward.

<u>*Improving your existing relationships*</u>

8) Write a list of things you'll no longer tolerate from your personal relationships.
    a. Write down things you dislike like being late, being disrespectful, etc.
    b. Commit to not allowing your personal relationships to conduct themselves in this manner around you.
9) Reduce/eliminate narcissistic behavior in your life.
    a. Commit to becoming a better listener and taking an interest in other people's lives.
10) Write out your "no" response and practice delivering it in the mirror.
    a. Use this response next time you receive an invitation that conflicts with other more important commitments.
11) Choose a day each week to call, hang out, and/or engage with someone you care about.
    a. Set a recurring alarm on your phone to ensure that you remember your commitment.

For a printable PDF list of these action items, check out the link below:

https://bit.ly/2B6k0gk

Chapter 5
Bookending your days

◆

"Routines are the ideal way to bookend your day. I think they are the building blocks of effectiveness, efficiency, and efficacy." – Mike Vardy

Each new day offers an opportunity to write a chapter of your life story. As we discussed previously, consistently making positive choices will compound your results over time. However, what can you do to ensure you consistently make the right choices each and every day? This is where the concept of "bookending your days" comes into play. Many of the most successful people in the world maintain productive morning and evening routines. Super achievers like Arnold Schwarzenegger, Richard Branson, and Bill Gates all credit their daily routines with helping them achieve their incredible success. In this section, we'll go over various activities you can incorporate into your daily routines and discuss the science behind each method.

Establishing a morning routine

"You'll never change your life until you change something you do daily. The secret of success is found in your daily routine." – John C. Maxwell

The morning is the quietist and most serene part of the day. So why is it that so many people have stress-filled mornings and feel rushed getting ready? Most often this can be attributed to lack of proper planning. Many people wake up late, don't give themselves enough time to complete their morning tasks, and then find themselves scrambling to get ready for the day. I've found the morning hours are my most productive hours and that performing my morning routine gives me the boost I need to start my day off right. What can you do to develop a routine that will set you up for a successful day? Let's go through some of my favorite activities:

Waking up earlier

One of the most impactful things you can do to improve your mornings is waking up earlier. Most people don't give themselves enough time in the morning to prepare for the day, and as a result find themselves scrambling to get ready. In the book, *Is Work Killing You?* by Dr. David Posen, Dr. Posen sites waking up late as one of the worst habits you can adopt. When you wake up late and rush through your morning, you put your body into a state of alarm, spiking your adrenaline and cortisol levels as soon as you get out the bed.[70] If these hormones are present at high enough levels for an extended period of time, they increase the risk of an array of degenerative diseases such as heart disease, ulcers, and Type 2 diabetes. Not only does waking up earlier help reduce stress levels, it can also have a positive impact on achieving career goals. In a study conducted by Christoph Randler of the Heidelberg University of Education, Professor Randler found that participants whose performance peaked in the morning were better positioned for career success because they were perceived to be more proactive than others who are at their best in the evening.[71]

I'm not saying you have to change your wake-up time from 7:00 a.m. to 5:00 a.m. right away. Many people who try to drastically change their wake-up time fall back into their old routine after a few days. A technique I used to establish and stick to an earlier wake-up time was setting my alarm clock back 15 minutes at a time. Once I maintained my new wake-up time for one week, I would set my alarm back another 15 minutes. I repeated this cycle until I finally got down to my desired wake up time of 5:00 a.m. The combination of setting my alarm back 15 minutes and holding that wake-up time for a week allowed me to smoothly transition to each new wake-up time, and I've stuck to it ever since. Try it out for yourself and see what a difference it makes in your mornings.

Making your bed

I adopted this routine after listening to the 2014 University of Texas commencement speech delivered by Admiral William H. McRaven. In his speech, Admiral McRaven talks about how making your bed each morning is one of the best things you can do to start your day. His logic is that by making your bed, you get your first small win of the day and build momentum towards accomplishing larger daily tasks. Not only that, but if you have an absolutely terrible day, you come home to a bed that is made and the satisfaction of knowing that tomorrow will be better. Since adopting this routine, I've had bad days that have physically and mentally drained me. However, when I come home and see my made bed, I'm overcome with a sense of great satisfaction. Along with these benefits, establishing a routine of making your bed each morning may help you appreciate life more.

In a survey conducted by hunch.com, a former website that helped people make decisions based on how they answered survey questions, 68,000 people responded to the question, *"Do you make your bed each morning?"* Of the 68,000 respondents, 27% said they made their bed each morning, 59% admitted they didn't, and 12% said they paid a housekeeper to do it for them. Part of the survey also asked how satisfied these individuals were with their day to day lives. The results showed that 71% of people who made their bed each morning reported being happy with their lives! At the other end of the spectrum, only 38% of people who didn't make their beds reported being happy with their lives.[46]

Although making your bed each morning may not directly lead to a happier life, other studies have shown that providing structure to your day can lead to a happier disposition. In the book *The Power of Habit* by Charles Duhigg, Charles explains how making your bed each morning is correlated with increased productivity, a greater sense of wellbeing, and increased likelihood of a person sticking to a budget. He also describes this habit as a "keystone habit," a habit which kickstarts a pattern of good behavior.[47] By getting your first task of making your bed accomplished for the day, you'll increase your motivation to complete many more. Set aside a few minutes each morning to make your bed and start your day off right. I promise that coming home to your made bed will be a welcome sight.

Meditating

Now, before you get skeptical about this routine, let me provide you with some insight. Meditation is a state of profound and deep peace that occurs when the mind is calm and silent.[76] This is a practice that has been utilized by many cultures around the world for millennia, and there's strong scientific evidence backing its health benefits. In a study conducted by the University of Wisconsin, scientists discovered that the practice of "Open Monitoring Meditation" reduced the gray matter density in areas of the brain related to anxiety and stress.[77] The less gray matter density a person has in these areas of the brain, the less stress and anxiety they experience on a day to day basis. This reduction in stress levels can significantly reduce the risk of heart disease, diabetes, and other chronic illnesses.

Along with the physical benefits associated with meditation, some of the mental benefits are quite intriguing. A study conducted by Katherine MacLean of the University of California found that subjects were more likely to stay focused on tasks during and after meditation training. This was especially true for tasks that were perceived to be repetitive and boring.[97] As someone who's always struggled focusing on one task for an extended period of time, the study struck a chord with me. Along with helping you sustain focus over time, other studies have shown that meditation can help increase cognitive performance.

One such study was conducted by researchers at the University of North Carolina at Charlotte. In the study, researchers found that students who performed 20 minutes of meditation per day were able to improve their performance on cognitive tests after just four days. On one particularly challenging computer test of sustained attention, students who practiced daily meditation performed 10 times better on the test than the control group. These students also significantly outperformed the control group on timed information processing tasks that were designed to induce deadline stress.[78] In other words, the students who practiced daily meditation were able to perform better under pressure than the control group. As someone who works in a profession that requires you to work well under pressure, this scientific study reinforced my desire to try out meditation for myself.

In June 2016, I decided to incorporate a guided meditation session into my morning routine. I usually dedicate the first five to ten minutes in the morning to meditation. Although many people perform meditation in silence, I prefer guided meditations. I've found that I have better meditation sessions when I have someone walking me through the process. I'm able to clear out all the thoughts in my head by zoning in on the guide's voice and focusing on my breathing. I use the app "Omvana" and utilize their free guided meditation sessions. Omvana is an app that provides free and paid guided meditation tracks to help support an effective meditation session. My favorite of the free guided meditation tracks is *Growing Your Light* by Gabrielle Bernstein. Try the app out for yourself and see what a difference it makes in your morning. I've provided the link to Omvana below. You can also search for the app on any Apple or Android device.

Omvana: http://www.omvana.com/

Having incorporated this practice into my morning routine and keeping with it for over two years, I can honestly say it's helped me perform better in various areas of my life. I feel more focused at work, I'm able to better reason through difficult problems, and I'm able to manage stress more effectively. Set aside five to ten minutes in the morning to get started with your meditation session. Don't worry if it's difficult at first. The most important thing is that you give yourself time to be still and silent.

Reading

As the great Ernest Hemingway often said, *"There is no friend as loyal as a book."* Reading a great book can open up new worlds for you. The knowledge and insight gained from each book you read can positively impact your life forever. Just over two years ago, I decided to incorporate reading into my morning routine. As a result, I've been able to read more than 50 non-fiction books over that timespan. Some of these books have helped me optimize my blog, establish healthy eating habits, develop an effective workout routine, improve as a software developer, and gain a broader understanding of various subjects. I'm confident that if I had not made reading a morning priority, you wouldn't be reading this book today. The insights I gained from reading these books nudged me to try new things and grow as a person.

One of my favorite types of books to read is biographies. I especially like to read biographies about people who dramatically changed the world for the better. Reading books about these successful individuals can have a profound effect on the way you view and approach future problems. Jim Rohn, the famous motivational speaker, noted that, *"You are the average of the five people you spend the most time with."* By reading biographies of successful people, you essentially get to spend time with them and absorb their views of the world. Over time you'll begin to adopt their success habits and see your life improve as a result.

Studies have also shown that a daily reading practice can help improve your memory. Reading a good non-fiction book requires you to remember an array of different information. Each time you establish a memory, new neural pathways are created. These neural pathways can be used to recall the information at a moment's notice. A unique thing about establishing new neural pathways is that it helps strengthen existing pathways as well.[75] It's a win-win situation! Try establishing a habit of reading five to ten pages of a good book each day. Over the course of a year, that will add up to between 10-20 two-hundred page books!

Journaling

About a year ago I decided to incorporate this habit into my daily routine. The therapeutic benefits of journaling have been well documented, and many of the most successful people of the modern era have admitted to keeping a journal. One of the many benefits of journaling is the effect it has on reducing your stress levels. In a study conducted at the University of Texas at Austin, psychologist and researcher James Pennebaker contends that regular journaling strengthens immune cells called T-lymphocytes and reduces stress hormones in the body. In other words, daily journaling about your emotions helps reduce stress levels and improves immune health.[76]

Journaling can also help you achieve lofty goals. In a study conducted by researchers at Harvard University, Harvard MBA students were asked a simple question: *"Do you write down your goals?"* Of all the students, 3% said they wrote down their goals, 13% said they took mental note of their goals, and 84% admitted to not having goals at all. After 10 years, the same groups of students were interviewed to see if goal setting had any impact on their success. The results of the study were astonishing. The 13% of students who took mental note of their goals but had not written them down were on average making DOUBLE the yearly income of the group of students who had no goals. The 3% of students who had consistently written down their goals were making, on average, **<u>10 TIMES</u>** more than the other 97% combined![79] The staggering difference in income between these three groups only reinforces the fact that writing down your goals, possibly in your journal, is an effective strategy that will culminate into future success.

Since January 2017, I've been utilizing *The 5-minute journal* as part of my morning routine. This resource is packed with inspirational quotes, calls to action and elegantly poses questions you can complete in less than five minutes each day. Since establishing this routine, I've seen substantial improvement in my performance at work and have made significant progress towards my goals for the year. I highly recommend this journal and have provided a link for it below:

<u>https://www.intelligentchange.com/products/the-five-minute-journal</u>

Exercising

Ah yes, the dreaded morning exercise routine. Although it may not be high on many people's priority list, an ever-growing number of research studies promote that it should be. Research suggests that morning exercise improves sleep and aids in the weight loss process.[80] Getting enough sleep is one of the most impactful things you can do to lose unwanted weight. This is because sleep helps rejuvenate the body and regulate your hormones. If you're sleep deprived for too long, your hormones can get out of whack and this can lead to added weight gain.

Performing an early morning exercise routine also positively impacts your metabolism. After a great workout, you experience Excess Post-Exercise Oxygen Consumption (EPOC). The term refers to the rate at which your body burns calories naturally without performing any form of exercise. This means that your body naturally burns more calories as you sit at your desk, drive your car, and/or perform other menial tasks throughout the day. One study even showed that participants who performed a rigorous workout routine burned an extra **190 calories** when compared to the control group in the 14 hours following their exercise routine![81] Let's explore what kind of impact this slight change can have on someone's life.

Imagine two people with the same 2,000 calorie diet. The first participant is placed in a group that exercises in the morning five times a week, while the other is placed in a non-exercise group. When the first participant performs a morning exercise routine, he/she burns 250 calories during that time period. If you add the 250 calories and the 190 calories experienced by EPOC, the participant would burn a total of 440 calories five times a week. Over the course of a year, this would translate to over 30 pounds of excess body weight! For many people who struggle with their weight, the effects this kind of weight loss would have on their self-confidence and overall health would be life changing.

Along with your increased metabolic rate comes increased attentiveness throughout the day. In an article titled *Be Smart, Exercise Your Heart: Exercise Effects on Brain and Cognition*, Dr. Charles Hillman and company explore the effects exercise has on our cognition. They concluded that exercise is associated with increased activity in portions of the brain responsible for higher order thinking.[82] The article suggests that participants who performed "difficult aerobic" exercises experienced the most benefits from the activity. In other words, if you want to perform well in tasks that require you to think critically, consider doing a challenging morning workout to start off your day.

In June 2016 I decided to incorporate a 10-15-minute exercise regimen into my morning routine. This regimen consists of body-weight exercises that focus on my upper body, lower body, and core muscles. In the *Bookending your days* resources section of the book, I've provided the workout regimen I utilized for two months (November 2017 to January 2018). Use this routine as a starting point as you incorporate your new exercise regimen into your morning.

Eating a healthy breakfast

An important part of starting your day off right is eating a healthy and nutritious breakfast. Your mother was right when she said breakfast is the most important meal of the day, and now there's science to back up her claim. A study conducted by Kings College in London suggests that although people who skip breakfast eat fewer calories to begin their day, they have higher Body Mass Indexes (BMI) than individuals who eat breakfast regularly. This increased BMI can be attributed to the fact that participants who skip breakfast feel hungrier throughout the day and tend to indulge more during lunch and dinner.[83]

What about those of you with a slower metabolism? Eating breakfast in the morning actually kickstarts your metabolism via a process referred to as diet induced thermogenesis (DIT). In this state, your body uses energy to digest and process the food you consume. When the food is higher in protein content, the burn rate can be as high as 15% of your daily energy expenditure![71] Along with an increase in metabolic rate, people who eat breakfast are generally more energetic. New evidence published in the *American Journal of Clinical Nutrition*, found that participants who were assigned to eat breakfast used more energy through physical activity than participants who were fasting.[84]

Although it's important to eat breakfast, not all breakfasts are created equal. Another study published in the *American Journal of Clinical Nutrition* analyzed a small group of obese females ages 18-20. In the study, half the participants were given a high protein breakfast to eat (35 grams) while the other half was given a low protein breakfast (13 grams). At the end of the day, participants who had eaten a higher protein breakfast reported feeling fuller throughout the day and did not indulge in as many snacks as the other group of participants. Subsequent brain scans further indicated that participants who ate breakfast had less brain activity in areas of the brain that controlled appetite.[85] I know that it may be hard for you incorporate a high protein/high fiber breakfast in the morning but adopting this beneficial habit will truly be a game changer. For some of my favorite breakfast options, check out the following article:

http://www.eatthis.com/high-protein-breakfasts/

Working on side projects

Have you ever wanted to start a passion project or create a side business? Through experimentation, I've found that the morning can be a great time to work on these activities. Since I wake up at 5 a.m., I'm able to allocate the first 45 minutes of the day to reading, exercising, and meditating. The rest of the morning I dedicate to tasks related to my growing side business. Utilizing this morning routine, I've been able to write two books and solicit three large speaking engagements over the course of seven months! Many great inventors and entrepreneurs have held down a job while burning the midnight oil. Although this works for some people, I've found that when I stay up late working on my side project, I feel groggy and unproductive the next morning. By going to bed earlier and using my mornings to be productive, I'm able to focus more intently on my work and as a result I produce a higher-quality product.

Various studies have shown just how beneficial being an early riser can be for improving productivity. In a 2008 study, Harvard biologist Christoph Randler found that students who considered themselves "early risers" were more likely to agree with statements such as, *"I spend time identifying long-range goals for myself"* and *"I feel in charge of making things happen."*[98] Other studies have shown how early risers tend to be much more proactive than their night owl peers. In a 1997 study led by veteran delay researcher Joseph Ferrari of DePaul, Joseph found that procrastinators were more likely to refer to themselves as "night" people. Based on six days of daily task records, Ferrari and company linked procrastination behaviors with a general tendency to partake in evening activities.[99]

In fact, you'll be surprised about how much you can actually accomplish over the course of a year utilizing this technique. While writing my first book, I dedicated about 90 minutes to writing each morning and would challenge myself to write at least 500 words during each session. Over the course of four months, I was able to write a 50,000-word book and dedicated over 120 hours of time to writing. That's over three weeks of full-time work! What side projects have you been looking to get started on? Consider setting aside time each morning to work on your side venture and see what you're able to accomplish!

Establishing an evening routine

"Evening is a time for real experimentation. You never want it to look the same way." – Donna Karan

As your day progresses, it can take on many forms. Some days may be filled with meetings, phone calls, and interruptions. Other days, you may have more time to focus on your most important goals and action items. Regardless of how it unfolds, ending your day with a solid evening routine will ensure that you continue building positive momentum that will set you up for success tomorrow. What are some of the most beneficial routines you can adopt prior to going to sleep? Below I've listed a few of my favorites.

Reviewing your wins and losses

Each day brings new triumphs and defeats. One day you may be riding high from winning a large contract with a big kahuna client, while on another day you may feel terrible about botching an important presentation at work. Taking some time at the end of each day to reflect on what you did well and what you can improve upon will set you up for a more successful tomorrow. In a study conducted by Harvard University professors Francesca Gino and Harry E. Figgie, 202 adults performed an online experiment where they were tasked with completing a series of brain teasers based on a "sum to ten" game.

Each round consisted of five problems where participants were awarded $1 for each problem they solved in 20 seconds or less. After the first round, researchers randomly assigned group members into three different groups: the control, reflection, and sharing groups. In the reflection group, participants took time to reflect on the previous round and write out detailed notes about the strategies they used to solve each problem. In the sharing group, participants received the same instructions as the reflection group but were also asked to share their thoughts with other group members. By the end of the study, the reflection and sharing groups both scored an average of 18% higher on subsequent problem-solving rounds than the control group.[23]

Not only that, but setting aside time each night to review your progress towards your goals can help improve your confidence. In a study conducted by Professor Therese Bouffard-Bouchard of the University of Quebec, Dr. Bouffard-Bouchard analyzed how self-regulation plays a role in building motivation and confidence. Self-regulation is composed of three related sets of activities. These are: self-monitoring, self-evaluation, and self-reactions. Self-monitoring provides us with information on how we're currently performing. Based on your perceived performance, you go through a period of self-evaluation where you analyze how your current performance lines up with the performance that will be required to reach your goals. Depending on your evaluation, you either respond with satisfaction or dissatisfaction (self-reaction). Over time, the compounded effect of these reactions either builds or destroys your confidence.[90]

As part of your evening routine, carve out some time to reflect on your day. What were some of your big wins? How did you go about solving these problems? Write out a few examples. Don't forget that it's also crucial to reflect on what you can improve upon in the future. What were some of the daily expectations you fell short of accomplishing? What actions can you take in the future to ensure you don't make the same mistakes again? I've been performing this routine for the past eight months and have experienced improvements in various areas of my life. Try this practice out for yourself and see what a difference it makes.

Planning out your next day

This is a new habit I just recently picked up. Although I specify my top three daily goals in my morning journal, I've also found it beneficial to write out my next day's most important tasks each evening. Our brains are wired to read and process metrics. Outlining the actions I'll perform the next day has helped me come up with innovative solutions to difficult problems in record time. This list operates as sort of "checklist" I use to tick off items as I complete them throughout the day.

In his best-selling book *The Checklist Manifesto*, Dr. Atul Gawande analyzes how using checklists can improve productivity, efficiency, and performance. In his own hospital, when a simple checklist was utilized and the staff introduced themselves to one another prior to surgery, the percentage of complications and deaths dropped by 35%![100] Not only that, but when the checklists were implemented in other hospitals around the country, they experienced equally miraculous results.

Given the value of outlining your most important daily tasks, commit to coming up with three of your own before you go to sleep each night. Why do I recommend three tasks? I've found that it's a number that pushes the limits of what you can accomplish each day, but it's not too big that you feel overwhelmed and eventually lose motivation. However, not all tasks are created equal. Writing down a task to check your email and surf the internet for a few hours is NOT a worthwhile task.

Your most important tasks must get you closer to accomplishing one of your yearly or long-term goals. The way I filter potential tasks is by utilizing Pareto's principle. Pareto's principle, as it applies to work productivity, states that 20% of the tasks you perform each day are responsible for 80% of your results. Therefore, you want to make sure that your top three tasks for the next day fall into that 20%. Developing this new habit, I've made significant progress towards my yearly and long-term goals! I hope that by continuing this routine for the rest 2018 and 2019, I'll be on pace to achieve my goal of writing four best-selling books by the end of 2019. Before bed, take a few minutes to make a list of your three most important tasks for the day ahead. You can block off time each night using the calendar functionality on your smartphone. Once you complete this routine, you can rest easy knowing that your next day is already planned out.

Expressing gratitude

In today's fast-paced society, it may feel almost impossible to stop our daily grind to appreciate the life we have. We live in the most prosperous time in human history and the abundance of opportunities to make a positive impact on the world is absolutely astounding. With all these options available to us, it can be easy to plough full steam ahead into every opportunity. However, we need to give ourselves permission to slow down and take time to reflect on the positives aspects of our lives. This is where the practice of "gratitude" comes into play. So, what is gratitude? The word gratitude is derived from the Latin word "Gratia," which means grace, graciousness, or gratefulness (depending on the context).[101] Although the practice of gratitude has been around for millennia, in recent years there have been many studies seeking to understand how the practice of gratitude effects overall wellbeing.

In a study conducted by professors Dr. Robert A. Emmons of the UC Davis and Dr. Michael E. McCullough of the University of Miami, the professors explored how the practice of showing gratitude affected a person's overall happiness. In the study, two groups of participants were tasked with writing out a few sentences about their day prior to going to sleep. The first group was instructed to focus on writing about things they were grateful for in life while the second group was tasked with writing about daily irritations or things that displeased them. At the end of the 10-week study, a survey was administered to each participant to determine their overall sense of happiness. The results showed that participants who had written about things they were grateful for each day were more optimistic and felt better about their lives. They also exercised more often and had fewer physician visits than those who focused more on their daily aggravations.[34]

One of the best times to practice gratitude is right before you go to sleep. This is because the day is winding down and you have time to reflect on your blessings. I recommend leaving a notebook by your bed and writing out three things you're grateful for each night. Some popular examples of things to be grateful for include being healthy, having a loving family, having supportive friends, having a fulfilling career, etc. By incorporating a practice of gratitude into your evening routine, you'll begin seeing the world in a more positive light and improve your overall wellbeing.

Reading a good book

Although I did recommend this practice in the *Establishing a morning routine* chapter, I feel it's also a great way to unwind after a long day. Reading an educational and/or inspirational book before bed gets you in the proper mindset to begin the day anew. Not only that but developing a routine of reading 10 pages of a good book before bed can add up to BIG results over time. Let's imagine you commit to reading 10 pages of a good book in the morning and another 10 pages before you go to sleep. If you only read on weekdays, you'll be able to finish one 200 page book every two weeks. That's around 24 books every year! If you maintain this routine for five years, you will have read almost 120 books! Do you think you'd be a completely different person after exposing yourself to that much positive content? Absolutely you will. If these books discuss subjects such as leadership, business development, entrepreneurship, management, engineering, etc., you'll have learned the equivalent of a PhD's worth of material. This would significantly increase your value in the marketplace and may even result in a life breakthrough.

Along with the educational and emotional benefits associated with reading, the physiological benefits cannot be ignored. Because we live in such an interconnected and technologically active society, many of us find it hard to pry ourselves away from our laptops and smartphones before bed. The blue light emitted from your cell phone and TV inhibits your body's production of melatonin.[3] This causes your body to take longer to fall into deep REM sleep. Since your body experiences the most rejuvenating sleep when you're in REM sleep, losing just one hour of REM sleep can cause you to feel groggy and irritable the next day. By reading a good book before bed, you limit your exposure to blue light and will find it easier to enjoy more restful sleep. As you start developing your evening routine, I strongly encourage you to consider implementing a reading session into your schedule. I promise you that your future self will thank you for it.

Going to bed earlier

As a compliment to waking up earlier, you should make it a goal to be in bed earlier. Establishing this new habit will help increase your alertness and attentiveness as well as support your long-term health. The results of a 2013 Gallup poll suggest that the average American sleeps around 6.8 hours per night. That's down almost a full hour from 1942.[73] Although we've become a more fast-paced society, we still need our sleep to perform at our best. Most physicians recommend that an average adult get between seven to nine hours of sleep per night. Since my wake-up time is 5:00 a.m., the latest I should be in bed is 10:00 p.m. You can use this baseline to set up your optimal bedtime.

What if you're already getting seven to nine hours of sleep? First off, congratulations! Although you may be getting seven to nine hours of sleep per night, not all nighttime hours are created equal. In the book *Sleep Smarter* by Shawn Stevenson, Shawn explains how the hours between 10:00 p.m. and 2:00 a.m. are our "money-time." These are the hours when our body experiences the most rejuvenating sleep. As soon as the sun starts to set, your body begins secreting melatonin (a sleep hormone). By the time 10:00 p.m. rolls around, your melatonin levels are high enough to promote your most rejuvenating sleep.[74] In order to ensure that I'm in bed asleep by 10:00 p.m., I've adopted the habit of getting into bed at least 30 minutes before my desired sleep time. Even though I may not fall asleep right when I get into bed, I've found that by establishing this routine I'm often asleep by 10:00 p.m. I now use this time to read a good book and write in my journal. Make the commitment today and experience how rejuvenated you feel in the morning.

Chapter 6
Developing positive habits

————————◆————————

"We are what we repeatedly do. Success is not an action but a habit." – Aristotle

This may be the most important chapter in the entire book. If you want to create a better life for yourself, you'll need to develop positive habits that support your new lifestyle. Success Coach Darren Hardy expressed it best when he said, *"Your life is a culmination of all the choices you've made and the habits you've developed up until this point in time."* So how do you go about developing positive habits that will lead you down the road to success while avoiding the many detours along the way? In this section, we'll go over strategies you can use to do just that.

Understanding the habit loop

"Motivation is what gets you started, a habit is what keeps you going." – Jim Rohn

Before incorporating or modifying any habit, it's important to first understand how habits are formed and how you can use the "habit loop" to your advantage. As described in Charles Duhigg's best-selling book *The Power of Habit*, the habit loop is a concept that plays a pivotal role in developing and maintaining habits over time. The habit loop consists of three distinct phases. The first phase is a CUE which triggers our brain to use a particular habit. The second phase is a ROUTINE, which is the action we perform as a result of the CUE. This action can be mental, physical, or emotional.

The final phase is the REWARD, which helps our brain determine whether a particular loop is worth remembering in the future. As time passes and the habit loop is repeated (Cue – Routine – Reward), a person's response to the cue becomes automatic. Eventually a habit is born and the brain stops fully participating in the decision-making process.

Breaking bad habits

When looking to change a bad habit, it's important to understand how CUES/TRIGGERS impact ROUTINES. Your cues will never go away, so the most effective way to change a bad habit is to change the routine associated with that cue. In the book, Mr. Duhigg chronicles the success of Alcoholics Anonymous in getting alcoholics to quit drinking. He explains how their focus on developing new routines for recovering alcoholics is the defining factor of their sustained success. Many alcoholics drink because it offers an escape from emotional turmoil, it relaxes them, it blunts anxiety, etc. (rewards). In terms of the habit loop, the emotions an alcoholic feels prior to drinking (anxiety, emotional turmoil, loneliness, etc.) are the "cues," and the results of drinking (companionship, blunted anxiety, etc.) are the "rewards." By replacing the routine of drinking with the routine of attending AA meetings and engaging with other alcoholics, AA was able to break the habit loop for millions of alcoholics around the world. The next time you decide you want to break one of your bad habits, be sure to focus on changing your ROUTINE. By doing so, you'll be well on your way to breaking your bad habit and implementing new, beneficial ones.

Building good habits from scratch

If you want to adopt a new beneficial habit, you'll need to define each phase of your new habit loop. First, determine what cue you'll use to trigger your desired routine. For example, when I wanted to incorporate writing into my morning routine, I defined my CUE as the alarm clock. Every morning when the alarm clock would go off, my ROUTINE was to immediately spring out of bed and begin my writing session. My REWARD was the two to three pages of solid content I had at the end of each writing session. Although your habit loop may be more complex than my example, take the necessary time to outline each phase. The time you spend defining your new habit loop will be well worth it.

Measuring your progress

Management guru Peter Drucker repeatedly said, *"What gets measured, gets managed."* Although this quote may have been intended for executives managing multi-national corporations, the same concept can be applied to developing beneficial habits. In his book *The 4 Hour Body*, Tim Ferriss encourages his readers to incorporate a workout regimen into their daily routine. As part of his plan, he suggests taking a "Before" picture and hanging it up somewhere you can consistently see it. Posting a "Before" picture on the wall gives you a base line off which to measure your progress. As his readers begin their new workout routines, Tim also encourages them to WRITE DOWN their workout plan and log their results. By measuring their progress over time, his readers are able to see the positive effects of their training and are motivated to push through the difficult workouts. On the other hand, if their results weren't to their liking, they'd have all the information they'd need to objectively look at their situation and tweak their process to improve future results.

Holding yourself accountable

As you continue refining your process of developing new habits, you'll find it's difficult to consistently hold yourself accountable. Now, before you get down in the dumps over it, know that it's completely normal to have issues with this. I consistently struggle with holding myself accountable to perform the positive routines that will help me achieve my goals. One of the best ways to ensure you get over the hump and solidify a newfound habit is to find an accountability buddy.

In a study conducted by the Department of Kinesiology at Indiana University, researchers surveyed married couples who joined health clubs together. They found that couples who went to the gym separately had a 43% dropout rate, while couples who went together, regardless of whether they focused on the same type of exercise, had only a 6.3% drop out rate![10] The substantial percentage difference between these two groups goes to show how impactful having a buddy can be. This principle can be applied to all habits and should be utilized to increase your odds of success. Ask a friend, family member, or a coach to be your accountability buddy. Just make sure they have the stomach to call you out when you don't stick to your end of the bargain.

It's also important to note that there are many great support platforms you can utilize to expedite the process of developing a new habit. One such platform is an app called *Weilos*. *Weilos* is a social media platform that connects users who are interested in sharing their weight loss and fitness goals. In a weight loss research study conducted by its founder, Ray Wu, Ray analyzed the weight change of users utilizing the app. He found that users who shared their weight loss goals and regularly provided selfies of their progress lost an average of 1.2 lbs. per week. That's more than a 400% improvement over the non-users (0.27 lbs. per week)![25]

When I decided to establish a morning writing routine, I made myself publicly accountable by sharing my desired habit via my blog and social media. By doing this, I introduced social pressure into the equation and as a result felt compelled to achieve my goal. I would have hated letting my family, friends, and colleagues down. Since establishing my new morning writing routine, I've written two books and have started my third. It's an extremely valuable exercise I highly recommend. In the *Developing positive habits* resource section of the book, I'll share some more insights on how to better hold yourself accountable to cement habits for good.

Sticking with it

Now that you've defined your new beneficial habit loop and found your accountability buddy, it's time to commit to sticking with your new routine until it becomes habit. In a study published in the *European Journal of Social Psychology*, Dr. Phillippa Lally and her research team decided to figure out just how long it takes to form a habit. A total of 96 participants were examined over a 12-week period to determine whether or not they stuck with their new behavior and how automatic the behavior felt over time. New habits varied and included habits as simple as *"drinking a bottle of water with lunch"* to *"running 15 minutes before dinner."* After 12 weeks, the researchers analyzed the data to determine how long each person took to adopt their new behavior. They concluded that it took them an average of 66 days to have their new behavior become automatic.[100]

This means that over the course of a year you could adopt around five new beneficial habits! These new habits could include going to the gym three to four times a week, eating healthier, reading, journaling, saving an extra 10% of your income, etc. Imagine where you'd be in a few years if you incorporated all these positive habits into your daily routine? I bet you'd be shocked. Make the commitment to start working towards developing a new positive habit today. It may take some time, but it will be well worth it.

Setting yourself up for success

"The first step towards getting somewhere is to decide that you are not going to stay where you are." – J.P. Morgan

When a construction worker decides to build a house, they first lay a strong concrete foundation to ensure the building can withstand the wear and tear it will experience on a daily basis. Similar to building a house, we too must establish a proper foundation prior to changing or creating any habit. Without a strong foundation, you'll find yourself falling short of your expectations. I've seen too many people decide they want to improve their lives only to fall back into their old habits when they don't see immediate results. What steps can you take to set yourself up for success? In this section, we'll delve into some strategies.

Stop relying on willpower

Have you ever wondered why it's difficult to stop yourself from indulging in tasty treats after a long day at work? I'll give you a hint: It's not because you were born with a sweet tooth. It has to do with a finite resource utilized by our brain to make decisions. This resource is called "willpower." Willpower is the ability to resist short term temptations in order to achieve long term goals. As we make decisions throughout the day, our willpower reserves slowly deplete. As your willpower drains, you'll find it increasingly difficult to choose between a satisfying option (e.g., cookies, cake, etc.) and an unpopular option (e.g., salad, exercise, reading, etc.) The more decisions, especially difficult ones, you make throughout the day, the harder it will be to resist temptations when they arise.

In fact, data compiled by Stanford professor Baba Shiv shows us just how fleeting willpower can be. In the study, professor Baba split 165 undergraduates into two groups and asked them to memorize either a two-digit or a seven-digit number. Both tasks were well within the average person's cognitive abilities and each participant could take as much time as they needed to memorize the sequence. Once the student was ready, they were transferred to another room where they would have to recall the number. Along the way, the subjects were offered a snack for participating in the study. The two snack choices were chocolate cake or a bowl of fruit salad (guilty pleasure vs. healthy treat). The results showed that students who were tasked with remembering the seven-digit number were TWICE as likely to choose cake as their snacking option.[14] The minimal disparity between the two sets of numbers just goes to show how easily willpower can be depleted. When attempting to adopt a new positive habit, it's important to eliminate as many external factors as possible. For example, if you're trying to eat healthier, get rid of all the junk food in your house. By doing this, you'll eliminate the temptation of snacking on unhealthy foods, which can deplete your willpower and lead you to make other poor decisions.

As you establish new beneficial habits, these routines will become automatic and will no longer require your focused attention. In a meta-analysis of various studies conducted by Brian M. Galla of the University of Pittsburgh and Angela Duckworth of the University of Pennsylvania, the professors analyzed how self-control affected willpower reserves. In the first study, the professors tracked participants' eating habits to determine how often they indulged in unhealthy snacks and meals. Although self-control did play a significant role in the decision-making process, the reason many participants refrained from making poor eating decisions is because they had established positive eating habits. Instead of relying on their willpower, their habits took over and the participants were able to control their urge to indulge. Not only did these principles apply to healthy eating, they also applied to various other areas. In five other studies, the professors were able to show that participants who established positive habits were more likely to maintain self-control over the duration of each study.[32]

What this means for us is that relying on willpower alone is a recipe for disaster. However, you can't relegate yourself to perpetual sorrow because you feel you don't have enough self-control to achieve your goals. What separates individuals who have self-control and those who don't are the positive habits they form over time. Establishing beneficial habits is the key to conserving your willpower so you can allocate the reserves to developing other beneficial habits. Examples of these habits include making a commitment to not allow unhealthy foods into your home, setting your alarm back 45 minutes to workout each morning, and setting aside time each night to write out your three most important tasks for the next day. By incorporating these rituals into your daily routine, you'll be able to perform your daily tasks without depleting your willpower. This will allow you to focus more of your energy on building beneficial habits that will serve you well in the future.

Thinking addition not subtraction

When people decide to adopt a new, positive lifestyle, they often focus on all the things they have to give up as a result. For example, if you're trying to lose weight and decide to remove foods that contain sugar and flour from your diet, you may focus on how you can no longer have cake or soda. If you're looking to save more money each month, you may focus on how you can't watch your favorite TV channel because you cancelled your cable subscription. If you decide you want to read more positive educational material each day, you may focus on how you don't have extra time to play *Call of Duty* with your friends each night.

Because you choose to focus on the things you "can't" have as a result of your decision, you reinforce your desires to pursue negative behaviors. Instead of focusing on the things you "can't" have (subtraction) start thinking about the things you "can" have (addition). Montel Williams, the host of *The Montel Williams Show*, illustrates this point beautifully. As a result of being diagnosed with Multiple Sclerosis (MS) in 1999, he was forced to modify his diet. Although he's no longer able to consume dairy, red meat, most grains, and sweets, he chooses to focus on the things he can have. These foods include fresh fruits and vegetables, avocados, fish, etc. By choosing to focus on the things he "can" have, Montel is able to maintain a positive disposition and even developed a new, positive habit. Now he loves his new diet and couldn't imagine life without it. Have you been focusing on the negatives surrounding your new positive habit? Try focusing on the benefits and see what a difference it makes. It may be just what you need to kick your motivation into high gear and cement your new habit for good.

Starting small

Rome wasn't built in a day. Neither were the pyramids of Giza, the Acropolis, Angkor Wat, or any other marvel of human history. They were built by laying one stone at a time. If the builders had resolved to build each structure in a week, they would have quickly lost motivation, and we wouldn't have these wonders to marvel at today. Just like these ancient builders, we must take small steps towards forming beneficial habits. One of the ways I've helped my clients maintain motivation over time is by encouraging them to focus on getting a few small wins initially. For example, if you're 50 pounds overweight, I don't recommend immediately switching to a diet of salad and saltine crackers, working out six days a week for 90-minute intervals, and making two sauna visits per day. This diet/exercise combination is not sustainable and will have you reverting back to your old ways in no time. Instead of going down this misguided path, I recommend taking a different approach. In the book *The Compound Effect*, Darren Hardy talks about how he helped his personal assistant, let's call her Debbie, run her first half marathon.

At the time, Debbie hadn't run a mile in over a decade and felt extremely out of shape. She was quite skeptical about ever being able to run three miles, let alone 13. Although this was the case, Darren started by asking her various questions about her motivations for running the half marathon. Understanding her motivations was extremely important because he wanted to help her craft the story she would reference when times were tough and she felt like quitting.

Once he uncovered that her reason for running the half marathon was *"wanting to look great for her high school reunion,"* Darren encouraged her to walk 1/8 of a mile three times that week. You may be thinking, *"Wow, that's it? That doesn't seem like much,"* but that's the point! Even though she only walked 3/8 of a mile over the course of a week, it was enough to get her into a rhythm of exercising and developing her positive habit without negatively impacting her motivation. Each subsequent week, Darren encouraged her to run until she felt out of breath. Once she felt out of breath, she was to immediately stop running and walk the rest of the way. After about two weeks, Debbie was able to run 1/8 of a mile without stopping. Although this may not seem like much progress, it was huge step in the right direction. She was encouraged by her positive results and was committed to continuing the routine. By increasing her running distance by 1/8 of a mile every few days, she was able to run nine miles without much effort a few weeks before the half marathon! The gradual increase of activity over time ensured that she stuck with her new routine and continued making positive choices that enabled her to reach her goals.

I utilized this exact strategy when I started my blog. In July 2016, I started a blog to help other Millennials find their way in the world. The blog is called *The Strong Professional,* and it focuses on topics related to personal development, professional development, exercise, healthy eating habits, and finances. At the time, I was extremely excited and wanted to write in-depth 1500 word posts every day. I was convinced I'd be able to maintain this writing pace while holding down a full-time job. However, after writing my first 1500-word post, I realized just how much effort was required to write one. It was then that I decided to write one detailed post every two weeks. This allowed me to get into a rhythm of writing consistently without overwhelming me right out of the gate. As a result of my decision, I've been able to maintain this schedule for almost two years, and I've created over 40 in-depth articles, penned two books, and produced over 100,000 words of unique content for my readers.

Celebrating the small wins

As you progress through the habit development process, you'll inevitably reach milestones along the way. As part of your success strategy, I highly encourage you to celebrate your small wins and reward yourself for your effort. It's tough implementing new positive habits and you deserve a pat on the back! In her book *The Progress Principle*, Harvard University professor Teresa Amabile seeks to understand how everyday life inside organizations can influence people and their performance. After one particular study where Dr. Amabile and her colleagues analyzed over 12,000 diary entries from 238 employees in seven companies, they discovered an intriguing pattern. The participants who tracked their achievements, however small, reported being happier and more motivated throughout the day.[102]

Whenever you run your first 5k, eat healthy for one week, or reduce your monthly spending by $100, treat yourself to something you enjoy doing. Research shows that positive reinforcement can actually change the makeup of your brain. In a process called neurogenesis, your nervous system tissue evolves and grows in response to stimuli in your environment. In one study, a group of rats in an enriched environment, one containing complex inanimate as well as positive social stimulation, experienced a five-fold increase in neurogenesis when compared to the control group.[103] Now you may be thinking, *"Raphael, I'm making a lot of progress towards my goals. How am I ever going to find the time and money to celebrate each of these milestones?"* These celebratory events don't have to be expensive or time consuming! Some ideas include reading one of your favorite books, taking a stroll through the park, eating at your favorite lunchtime spot, etc. Just make sure you actually enjoy the event and remember to always celebrate the small wins. With this strategy in place, you'll be well on your way to implementing new positive habits.

Chapter 7
Creating S.M.A.R.T. goals

◆

"A dream is just a dream. A goal is a dream with a plan and a deadline." – Harvey Mackay

Setting goals is an important part of achieving success in anything you do. Whether your goals are work related, personal, or spiritual, structuring your goals effectively can drastically increase the probability of you achieving them. In this section, I'll challenge you to outline your optimal life, show you how to effectively structure your goals to increase your likelihood of achieving them, and go over strategies you can utilize to compound your positive results over time.

Outlining your optimal lifestyle

We all know that writing down your goals can help move you closer to the life you want. However, what does this "optimal" life look like? When I ask my clients this question, they often respond with a blank stare. It's easy to get caught up in the day to day grind without taking a step back to evaluate what you want from life. Amazingly, when my clients actually stop and think about where they want to go, they sometimes realize they've been going down the wrong path altogether. Although this can be a relief for some, others kick themselves for not seeing it sooner.

To avoid this heartache in the future, I suggest defining what's most important to you in life. Is it your family? Your friends? Your job? How will you prioritize them? Along with asking yourself these questions, it's important to understand the opportunity costs associated with each decision you make. It's easy to set lofty goals for yourself and not realize the sacrifices you'll need to make to achieve them. Writing down a goal of becoming a Fortune 500 CEO seems like an awesome goal until you witness the consistent 70-80 hour weeks, days away from family, and extreme stress you'll face on the job. Jim Rohn often said that by choosing to focus on one of your goals, you're unable to focus on other areas of your life. This is in no way meant to discourage you from setting lofty goals. I regularly set seemingly unattainable goals for myself to push my limits. However, I understand that I'm sacrificing other opportunities as a result. Using this idea as your foundation, sit down and create an outline of your optimal life. Below I've provided a few questions to get you started. Be sure to take time to answer each question thoroughly and come up with a few of your own:

1) *Where do you live?*
2) *Do you have a spouse?*
3) *Do you have children?*
    a. *How many do you have?*
4) *What's your job/career?*
    a. *Do you travel regularly?*
5) *What does your financial situation look like?*
6) *What are your hobbies?*
7) *How many days off do you have per year?*
8) *How many hours do you dedicate to work, family, friends, and faith?*
9) *What do the people in your life think about you?*
    a. *Family?*
    b. *Friends?*
    c. *Collogues?*
10) *What charities and/or causes do you regularly support?*

In the *Creating S.M.A.R.T. goals* resource section of the book, I've provided my optimal life outline as an example. Now that you have your completed outline in hand, let's take a look at how to craft compelling goals that fit within your life plan. As a frame of reference, I've provided my 2017 goals to show you how to structure your goals using the S.M.A.R.T. goal-setting technique:

Raphael's 2017 goals:

1) I will run the Punta Cana Marathon on April 2, 2017. To accomplish this goal, I will run at least five miles three times a week. One month before the race, I will increase my running length to 10 miles at least twice per week and between five to seven miles two times a week. I will run a half marathon March 12, 2017, in Puerto Rico to prepare for my full marathon.

2) I will perform at least one paid speaking engagement by August 15, 2017. I will accomplish this by attending every Toastmasters meeting to refine my craft and send at least two emails per week to organizations looking for speakers.

3) I will be consistently making an extra $1,000 per month on the side by September 15, 2017. I will do this by sending out at least five job requests per week on Thumbtack, Fiverr, and/or Upwork. I will also develop paid coursework that I'll offer to my clients.

4) I will build an email list of at least 5,000 people by December 15, 2017. I will do this by committing at least $25 per week to use Google AdWords to drive traffic to my landing page. I will experiment with A/B testing so I can increase my conversion rate to over 50%.

5) I will write my first book this year and have the rough draft completed by May 15, 2017. I will accomplish this by writing at least 500 words per weekday for five months (50,000 words). Once I have my rough draft complete, I will revise the draft and have a final draft ready to publish by July 15, 2017.

6)   I will speak at least six times this year and have at least two of those speeches be completely in Spanish. I will accomplish this by attending every Toastmaster's event and volunteering for every opportunity to speak in front of the members. I will also email SHPE, Engineers 4 Business, Entrepreneurs@ASU, and other organizations I've been a part of to see if they need guest speakers. This will all be accomplished by November 15, 2017.

S stands for Specific

When defining your goal, it's important to make it as specific as possible. What do you want to accomplish? Who is involved? Where is it located? By asking yourself these questions, you'll start to craft a tangible goal that you can begin striving towards. In my marathon example, I describe the fact that I will run the *"Punta Cana Marathon on April 2, 2017."* This level of specificity allows me to envision running that specific marathon and puts me on a path to achieve that goal.

M stands for Measurable

Metrics are the life blood of any goal you want to accomplish. If you don't have any kind of metrics tied to your goal, how do you know if you're on track to achieve it? By defining at least one metric, you'll be better able to determine if you're on track to achieving your desired outcome.

In my example of writing a book, I specified that I would write *"500 words per weekday for five months."* This gave me the opportunity to measure if I was in fact on track to hit those numbers. If by February 15 I'd only been able to write 5,000 words, I could have done the math to find out how many words I'd have to write daily to catch up to my baseline. This extremely powerful tool should not be ignored, and you should take some time to define some good metrics to adhere to.

A stands for Attainable

A great question to ask yourself is, *"Will I be able to achieve these goals in the timeframe I've set for myself?"* I've met many enthusiastic/ambitious people who have huge dreams for themselves but struggle accomplishing their goals because their goals are not attainable in the timeframe they've allotted for themselves.

For example, you're an aspiring restaurateur who writes a goal of opening 15 restaurants by the end of the year. Although I commend you on your ability to think big, this goal is probably not achievable in the timeframe you've specified. A more attainable goal would be to open up your first location and achieve $X desired revenue for the year. Not only is this goal achievable, it also has a metric tied to it that will help you determine if you're on track to achieving your goal. The lesson here is to not be afraid to stretch your abilities and dream big but also have realistic expectations given a particular timeframe.

R stands for Relevant

This section can be confusing for some people. When a goal is relevant, that means it applies to your bigger purpose in life. Do you want to be a high-level manager in an organization? Are you trying to be the best significant other or friend you can be? Do you want to help others with your message? Make sure your goals line up with what you want to accomplish in life. In my example of my "paid speaking engagement" goal, I hope to one day speak to people around the world, spreading my message of living an efficient life. Being hired for a paid speaking event will steer me towards realizing that dream.

T stands for Time-Bound

Like all great goals out there, it's important to have a deadline for achieving them. Without a set deadline, people naturally lose motivation and procrastinate on performing the actions necessary to achieve their goals. Every single one of my goals has a set date of completion. This makes it easier for me to use my metrics to see if I'm on track to achieving my goals by their deadline.

Another helpful tip when setting timelines for your goals is to stagger their due dates. As you accomplish each one of your goals, you'll gain more confidence and build momentum that will propel you towards achieving the next one. However, don't be discouraged if you don't meet your goal by the deadline. It's important to sit down and evaluate where you are and what needs to be done to get you back on track. When you come up with a solution, you'll then set a new target date and begin working towards it like before.

Congratulations on making it this far! The mere fact that you've thought about your goals puts you in the top 20% of the population! Now that you know how to structure S.M.A.R.T. goals, spend some time writing out a few of your own. By writing out your goals, you'll join the top 3% of the population who write out their goals. Believe me when I say that the time spent outlining your goals will be time well spent.

Sharing your goals and progress with others

Now that you've written out your S.M.A.R.T. goals, you'll want to share them with others via mediums such as social media, your own personal blog, stickk.com, etc. By sharing your goals with the world, you introduce a level of accountability that will improve your likelihood of success. As stated in the *Developing positive habits* section of the book, we're more likely to stick to our resolutions when we know others are watching. In fact, one study shows just how powerful sharing your goals and sending regular progress updates can be.

When participants merely took mental note of their goals and thought about how to reach them, they succeeded in doing so less than 50% of the time. However, when participants wrote down their goals, shared them with others, and sent regular progress updates to accountability partners, they were able to achieve their set list of goals around 75% of the time.[36] As the study indicates, sharing your goals with others can substantially increase your likelihood of achieving your goals. I suggest that as you reach particular milestones, send out updates to friends, family members, and/or your coach. You can do this by sending a text, calling, and/or sharing an update via social media. Not only will this practice increase your likelihood of success, acknowledging your progress will motivate you to keep moving forward. When I finalized my 2018 goals, I printed them out and hung up them up on my bedroom wall. I also shared my goals with my coach, created a post on my blog *The Strong Professional,* and posted various status updates on social media. As I hit milestones throughout the year, I celebrated my progress with my coach and on my blog. Try this technique out for yourself and see how much more you'll be able to accomplish this year.

Reviewing your goals

"Failing to plan is planning to fail." – Alan Lakein

As the year progresses, I find that reviewing my progress towards each of my goals is extremely beneficial. This is important for two reasons. First, it gives me the opportunity to celebrate the progress I've made. Research shows that having a sense of making progress towards your goals is the most important factor in maximizing long-term creative output, positive emotions, and motivation.[85]

Second, I'm able to see where I'm falling short of expectations and can adjust my effort accordingly. For example, in 2017 when I performed my first quarterly review I realized that I had not put enough effort into delivering six presentations by the end of the year. After the review, I sought out opportunities to present wherever I could and subsequently hit my goal later in the year. Had I not objectively analyzed my progress during my first quarterly review, I would have fallen farther behind and may have missed the mark altogether. There's extreme value in taking time to review your goals. Review cycles vary, but I recommend my clients perform weekly, quarterly, and annual reviews. In the following section, we'll go through each type and I'll explain what to look for.

Weekly review

It's the end of a difficult week and you're glad it's finally over. You can now kick up your feet, grab a good book, and relax. However, it's also important to set aside a few minutes to evaluate what progress you've made towards your monthly, quarterly, and yearly goals. For example, while I was writing my first two books in 2017, I would review my weekly word count and determine whether or not I was on track to complete the books by their deadlines. If I was falling behind on my word count, I could increase the number of words I wrote the following week to get back on track.

By performing this routine, I was able to stay on track and eventually finished both my books ahead of schedule! Although you probably see the value of this routine, you may be wondering, *"Raphael, how much time will this take per week? It seems like a significant time commitment and lot of work!"* We all have extremely busy schedules, and the thought of committing to evaluating your goals each week may seem unappealing. However, this process should take no more than 10-15 minutes. You should focus your attention on the metrics you established for each of your S.M.A.R.T. goals and measure how you did for the week. If you met or exceeded your expectations, congratulations! Keep up the good work. However, if you fell short of expectations, you'll need to determine what action you need to take to get back on track. This routine is immensely beneficial and I highly recommend it.

Quarterly review

No surprise here, quarterly reviews occur at the end of every quarter (March, June, September, and December). This review is generally more in depth than your weekly review and will take between 45 minutes to one hour to complete. During this session, you'll want to focus on celebrating your wins for the quarter, creating a plan of attack to improve in areas where you fell short of expectations, and reassessing your one to three-year goals to ensure they still align with your values.

For example, during my first evaluation, I celebrated having written 30,000 words for the first draft of my book! It was a big accomplishment and I was extremely proud of myself. Next, I focused on creating a plan of attack to get me closer to my goal of delivering six presentations in 2017. In the plan, I determined I needed to schedule times to present at my local Toastmasters and send out emails to various university clubs to see if they needed speakers. Finally, I evaluated my one to three-year goals to see if they aligned with my greater purpose in life. Since I want to eventually transition into becoming a full-time author, speaker, coach, and entrepreneur, I concluded that the progress I made towards my goals was moving me closer to this reality.

Yearly review

The year has come to a close and you're getting ready to ring in the New Year. Although this is a time for celebrating new beginnings, it's also a time to reflect on past accomplishments and shortcomings. What I like to do at the end of each year is review my yearly goals and outline how I measured up. This gives me a framework off which to define my goals for the new year. I've provided an outline of my 2017 goals in review as a reference:

Running a marathon

    I completed my first marathon on April 2, 2017, in Punta Cana, Dominican Republic. Leading up to the race I hurt my foot while finishing a 10-mile run. I was nervous the day of the race because I didn't know if my foot would hold up. Luckily, I was able to complete the race in 5:03 hours and I can now cross this goal off my bucket list. It's definitely a phenomenal experience and I encourage more people to try it out.

Writing a book

The title of my first book is *The Millennial Playbook: Proven Success Strategies for the Millennial Generation*. Although I started the year writing a substantial amount of content, my enthusiasm wavered and effort slowed around mid-March 2017. By early May I only had 35,000 words written! For the next month I dedicated myself to writing at a feverish pace, and I eventually hit my goal of 50,000 words on June 1st. I reviewed the book three times myself before sending it off to a professional editor. I also contracted a local Puerto Rican graphic artist to design the book cover and bought a group of 10 ISBN numbers.

I finalized my book on August 10, 2017 and released it to the public a few months later! As of March 2018, the book has been purchased/downloaded over 300 times and has been featured in various media publications. You're also reading the completed version of this book (my second), and I'll be referencing it in my 2018 yearly review!

Delivering six speeches (two in Spanish)

This is a goal I also completed relatively early in 2017. As part of Toastmasters International, a nonprofit educational organization that operates clubs worldwide for the purpose of helping members improve their communication, public speaking, and leadership skills, I delivered nine speeches in 2017 (three completely in Spanish). I also facilitated a Q&A presentation for a club I started in college and delivered a technical work presentation to a group of 25 developers completely in Spanish. I completed this goal on August 2, 2017, when I gave my second speech of the year in Spanish. For a video of the speech, check out the link provided here: https://www.youtube.com/watch?v=MFzyaLSeANg

Making an extra $1000 per month

This is one of the goals I stalled on. I focused most of my attention on finishing my first book and as a result didn't generate much income on the side. With both books now available on Amazon, I've started seeing extra income come in every month in the form of book royalties. Also, after hurricane Maria ravaged the Caribbean in September 2017, I decided to donate 100% of the proceeds from my first book to hurricane relief efforts.

As a result, we've been able to raise over $1000 for charities helping in the Caribbean. I recently committed to sending out 3-5 speaking inquiry emails each day and have been regularly attending networking events in Louisville. I'll be incorporating these metrics into my 2018 financial S.M.A.R.T. goals.

Securing a paid speaking engagement

Raphael E. Collazo

Life Coach, The Strong Professional
Implementation Consultant, FAST Enterprises

Raphael is a software implementation consultant for FAST Enterprises currently working on the SURI Project in San Juan, Puerto Rico. His responsibilities include working with the Puerto Rican Department of the Treasury to outline complex business processes and develop the GenTax commercial off the shelf software system (COTS) to fit their needs. Previously, he was a software implementation team member on the Modern Integrated Tax System project (M.I.T.S) in Washington D.C for the Individual Income tax software roll out.

Raphael has been engaged with numerous organizations including Toastmaster, Boys and Girls Club, Engineers for Business and Society of Professional Hispanic Engineers. Through these organizations, Raphael has provided his expertise to help develop and grow the membership of each organization.

Raphael is a frequent speaker at local organization events as well as conferences focused on engineering, business and entrepreneurship. He is the self-published author of the "Millennial Playbook" whose subject matter centers on helping millennials improve in 5 areas of their life. These areas are personal development, professional development, healthy eating habits, finances and exercise. He also runs a blog (www.thestrongprofessional.com) where he provides content related to the previously mentioned subject matter. Raphael loves music, dancing, travelling and speaking to professionals about improving their life.

This is another one of my goals that I didn't dedicate much time to accomplishing. Although I had various speaking engagements throughout the year, none of them were paid. In response to my lack of results, I added a "Speaking" page to my blog and website and created a speaking bio (see picture above) to send out to prospective clients. I also began making inquiries to local businesses to see if they needed speakers for upcoming events. I've also hired a speaking and publishing coach to hold me accountable for soliciting more speaking engagements. As a result of my efforts, I was able to book several large speaking events and I'm hopeful I'll book my first paid speaking engagement by the end of 2018.

Acquiring 5000 email subscribers

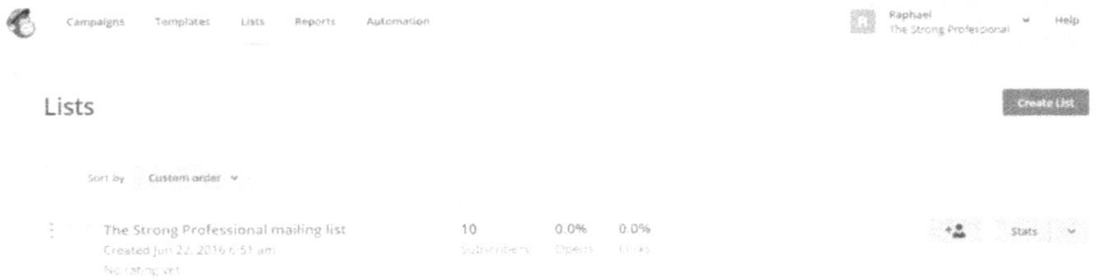

Over the course of 2017, the Strong Professional acquired a total of… (drum roll)…10 email subscribers. Although this is a paltry number, I did make steps during the year that increased my total. I reached out to four or five different blogs with higher traffic to see if I could guest post for their blog. One of the blogs responded, and I was able to post one of my articles on the site. It received over 3000 views and resulted in a few email subscribers. If you want to check out the article, I've provided a link here: (https://www.dumblittleman.com/how-to-get-a-raise/). I also set up a Google AdWords account and went through the initial process of defining what keywords I would bid on for my marketing campaign.

Once you've completed this exercise, revise your existing plan of attack to better help you reach your yearly goals. As stated in the *Creating S.M.A.R.T. goals* section of the book, be sure to assign metrics to your new goals to make it easy to understand what it will take to reach each goal.

Creating your vision board

"The only thing worse than being blind is having sight but no vision." – Helen Keller

Now that you've written out your yearly goals, it's time to create your vision board. However, you may be wondering, *"Raphael, what's a vision board?"* A vision board is any sort of board on which you display images and quotes that represent whatever you want to be. Every vision board is unique and should line up with your core values. Utilizing a vision board taps into the power of visualization. As we discussed in previous sections, studies have proven the power of visualizing your goals.

One such study conducted by Guang Yue, an exercise psychologist from the Cleveland Clinic Foundation in Ohio, compared participants who worked out at a gym to others who performed mental workouts. At the end of the 12-week study, Guang found that participants who physically worked out experienced a 30% strength increase while the group who performed mental weight training exercises experienced a 13.5% strength increase.[88] That's almost half the results without even physically performing the exercise!

Not only that, but these results persisted for three months after the participants stopped performing the mental workout. Imagine if you combined visualization with deliberate action towards your goals. Your results could be compounded. So how do you go about creating a compelling vision board? Below I've provided step by step instructions.

What are your intentions?

Before adding anything to your vision board, you'll want to set aside time to come up with answers to the following questions:

1) *What are your values?*
    a. *What's most important to you in life?*
2) *What do you desire?*
    a. *Items, lifestyle, etc.*
3) *What do you need?*
    a. *Home, family, friends, etc.*
4) *How will attaining your goals make you feel?*

For example, if you want to own a Lamborghini, you may want to attach a picture of a person driving a Lamborghini to your vision board. If you desire a happy family life, maybe attach a picture of a happy family spending time together. I suggest referencing your yearly S.M.A.R.T. goals for inspiration of what to attach to your vision board.

Gathering your supplies

Now that you've determined what your intentions are, it's time to gather the necessary supplies for creating your vision board. Below I've provided a list of the supplies you'll need:

- ☐ *Blank art book/poster board/a large sheet of paper, and/or a cork board*

- ☐ *Glue/pins*

- ☐ *Markers, pens, paint*

- ☐ *Colorful or plain paper*

- ☐ *Magazines/books that can be cut up (some popular magazines are* Success, Inc, Forbes, Vogue, Life, *etc.)*

- ☐ *Scissors*

For a complete list of supplies, check out the link provided here: (http://astore.amazon.com/visionboardblog-20?_encoding= UTF8&_node=2). When searching for pictures and quotes, it's important to compile photos and quotes that will inspire you to pursue your aspirations. You'll also want to visualize what your life will be like once you've achieved each vision on your board. For example, if you attach a picture of a Lamborghini, you'll want to envision the exhilaration of driving the car and/or visualize the rush of wind in your face as you slam your foot on the accelerator.

This same logic should apply to your quotes as well. One of the quotes I attached to my vision board was delivered by Winston Churchill. The quote reads, *"Success is stumbling from failure to failure with no loss of enthusiasm."* Whenever I read this quote I'm reminded that even though I may face setbacks throughout the day,

I should continue to be enthusiastic because I know there will be a better tomorrow. This mindset will be crucial as I seek to attain my goal of becoming an internationally renowned author, entrepreneur, and public speaker.

Building your board

You've sifted through magazines, newspapers, and/or surfed the internet to find pictures and quotes that resonate with you. You're now ready to create your vision board. Next, you'll want to find a space where you feel comfortable working on your board. A large table or a space on the floor usually works best. I also recommend choosing soothing background music to play as you work. Recent studies have shown that listening to background music while performing creative work increases "divergent thinking." This kind of thinking is necessary to maximize creative output and will help you create a compelling vision board.[89] Now that you have your space picked out and your music playing, spread out your supplies on the surface. Begin attaching/pinning your pictures, quotes, and other objects to your board. Repeat this step until your board is full of inspiring content.

Hanging up your vision board

Now that you've built your vision board, I recommend hanging it somewhere you can regularly see it. Just as it's beneficial to hang up your written goals, it's also beneficial to hang up your vision board. In a study conducted by Professor John Hattie and Helen Timperley, the professors examined how instructing students affected overall academic performance. They found that when instructors set explicit learning goals and students had a clear picture of course expectations, they were better able to concentrate their efforts efficiently towards their attainment.

This focused effort translated into better academic performance and an increased likelihood of seeking feedback from professors.[58] In other words, having a clear picture of your goals will increase the likelihood of you actually achieving them. I've hung my vision board in my room, and it's one of the first things I look at in the morning. Doing this helps me maintain my motivation and compels me to make my visions a reality.

Finding an accountability partner

We all know the importance of having an accountability partner when pursuing lofty goals. In the *Creating S M.A.R.T goals* section of the book, I referenced how spouses who regularly attended the gym together were much more likely to stick to their new habit than couples who attended the gym separately.[53] If this is true for S.M.A.R.T. goals, why can't it be true for vision boards? When searching for an accountability partner, you'll want to ask someone you feel comfortable seeking feedback from but also someone who won't be afraid to call you out when you stray off course. This person can be your significant other, family member, coach, and/or a close friend. As you move toward each goal, either send them an update via text, a phone call, a message via social media, or mentioning it to them in person. Eventually, you'll begin to see the goals on your vision board become a reality.

Creating my vision board

At first, I was skeptical about creating a vision board. I'm not the artsiest person in the world and I didn't think I could come up with something that really captured my goals on a single piece of cardboard. However, after reading an article about how effective vision boards can be, I decided to give it a shot. I've provided the link to the article here:

https://www.huffingtonpost.com/elizabeth-rider/the-scientific-reason-why_b_6392274.html

I enlisted the help of my girlfriend and together we set out to create our own unique vision boards. The start of the process was a little messy. I remember there were pieces of paper everywhere, and I'm pretty sure 30-40% of my body was covered in glue! However, after having put all the articles, pictures, and quotes on my vision board, I can honestly say that I felt a strong sense of accomplishment. We decided to hang up our vision boards in our bedroom and we now look at them every day. As the months have passed I'm amazed at how many of the visions on my board have come true. One of the pictures on the board was this very book that you're reading right now! I'm excited to see how many more of the visions on my board become a reality.

Taking action

Although a vision board will be the visual representation of the goals you want to accomplish, it's a relatively ineffective tool unless it's coupled with deliberate action. As we discussed in *The choices you make* section of the book, performing actions that move you closer to your goals each day will help build momentum. These small wins will eventually lead to massive breakthroughs in your life. On top of that, taking time to monitor your progress will ensure that you sustain this success.

In a study published in the *Psychological Bulletin*, University of Sheffield's Dr. Benjamin Harkin sought to understand how monitoring progress affected a person's likelihood of achieving lofty goals. In the study, Dr.Harkin and his colleagues analyzed 138 studies comprised 19,951 subjects. These studies focused primarily on personal health goals such as losing weight, quitting smoking, changing diet, lowering blood pressure, etc. The results showed that prompting individuals to monitor their progress increased their likelihood of achieving a goal. Not only that, but the more frequent the participants monitored their progress, the more likely they were to achieve it.[105]

Whether it's writing X amount of words each day if you're an author, saying I love you to your significant other if you want to be a better boyfriend/girlfriend, or reaching out to an extra three prospects each day if you want to grow your business, be sure to specify what your action is and monitor your progress. You can drastically improve your focus areas over time if you consistently perform your key daily actions.

Action Items

Establishing a morning routine

1) Commit to waking up at least 30 minutes earlier in order to incorporate a new morning routine.
2) Incorporate at least 3 of the strategies discussed in this section into your morning ritual.

Establishing an evening routine

3) Dedicate at least 30 minutes every evening to perform your evening routine.
4) Incorporate at least 3 of the strategies discussed in this section into your evening ritual.

Developing positive habits

5) Commit to implementing one positive habit into your daily routine over the next 3 months.
   a. Focus on making subtle changes at first and eventually work your way up to bigger habits.
6) Commit to eliminating one bad habit from your routine over the next 3 months.
   a. Define your "habit loop" and seek to replace your "routine" with something more positive.
7) Find an accountability buddy.
   a. Commit to sending weekly text updates to your buddy outlining your progress.

Creating S.M.A.R.T. goals

8) Write out 3-5 yearly goals using the S.M.A.R.T. goal setting system.
   a. Once complete, share your goals on social media.
9) Use http://www.stickk.com/ to help you reach one of your most important goals.

a. Enlist the help of a friend to be the mediator.

10) Set an alarm on your phone to review your progress each quarter (every 3 months).

11) At the end of each year, review your goals and determine your wins and losses. Apply those lessons to designing your future S.M.A.R.T. goals.

Creating your vision board

12) Make a weekend trip to your local arts and crafts store to purchase supplies for your vision board.

   a. For a list of supplies, review this section.

13) Elicit the aid of a friend, family member, and/or significant other to help you create your vision board.

   a. Pick a date and time to create your vision board. Set an alarm for this event on your smartphone.

14) Once complete, hang your vision board somewhere you can see it regularly.

   a. Each morning, take a moment to look at your vision board and visualize attaining your goals.

15) Set an alarm on your phone to review your progress towards your vision board goals each quarter (every 3 months).

For a printable PDF list of these action items, check out the link below:

https://bit.ly/2Bc9SCS

Chapter 8
Building confidence

◆

"I am the greatest; I said that even before I knew I was." - Muhammed Ali

It was February 1964 in Miami Beach, Florida, and two heavyweight powerhouses were set to go toe to toe in one of the most anticipated fights of the century. Sonny Liston was the reigning heavyweight champion and known for his ferocity in the ring. His opponent was an up and coming fighter from Louisville, Kentucky, who had been trash talking Liston in the weeks leading up to the fight. Confidence exuded from him, and it was obvious to everyone that this young man believed in his ability. On the night of the fight, Sonny Liston was a 7-1 favorite. The boxing community had already written off his opponent and many were predicting a first-round knockout in favor of Sonny Liston. What eventually happened that night would change the boxing world forever. Contrary to what was expected, Sonny received a boxing lesson and eventually folded in the seventh round of the fight. That night a new heavyweight champion of the world was crowned. The 21-year-old's name was Cassius Clay, also known as Muhammed Ali.

Ali credited much of his success in the ring to his unwavering confidence. He was certainly a dominant fighter with a rare combination of speed and strength, but his true advantage was his confidence. He often got into his opponent's head even before the fight took place. Although you may not be climbing into the boxing ring any time soon, one of the most beneficial things you can do to improve your overall success in life is to develop confidence in yourself and your abilities. If you look at the great achievers of our generation, they're all extremely confident. They use this confidence to face down adversity and pursue their vision even when doubt and fear creep in. But how do you go about building that type of confidence? In this section, we'll explore different strategies you can use to help you do just that.

The 4 C's of confidence

"Believe you can and you're halfway there." – Theodore Roosevelt

Over the past few years, I've sought to uncover how to develop confidence in various areas of my life. I've done this by reading countless books on the subjects of personal development, leadership, management, and psychology. I've also studied many successful individuals who exhibit a high degree of confidence in their day to day lives. and by studying individuals who exhibit a high degree of confidence. What I discovered was that there are four distinct parts of the confidence building process. These are what I like to call *"the 4 C's of confidence."* Below I've highlighted each part of the process.

Courage

This word often elicits comparisons to the men and women who put their lives on the line for the good of our country. Although military and law enforcement personnel are some of the most courageous individuals in our society, you don't need to be one of them to be courageous in what you do. What I mean by "courage" is not being afraid to put yourself out there and opening yourself up to failure. It's the first step of the confidence building process because being courageous opens you up to try new things. By making the decision to try something new, you begin the process of developing new skills and growing your confidence.

Examples of these decisions include taking a promising job opportunity in a city you've never been before, meeting an attractive woman/man at a mixer and asking them out on a date, starting a business even though you have to leave your cushy job to do so. Every one of these decisions requires courage because failure is a strong possibility. Although this is the case, the rewards these opportunities provide can be life-changing. There will be many opportunities that pass you by if you choose the safe and well-worn path as your default option. The trailblazers in various industries, such as Walt Disney, Steve Jobs, Oprah, and Henry Ford, took a chance on something they felt passionate about even though the likelihood of failure was very high.

Next time a promising opportunity comes your way, whether it's financial, personal, professional, or health related, flex your "courage" muscle and jump into the opportunity head first. Even if it leads to failure, remember the famous quote given by Jon Wooden, one of the greatest coaches of all time, which reads: *"Success is never final, failure is never fatal, it's courage that counts."*

Consistency

An aspiring young comic once asked Jerry Seinfeld what it took to become a world class comedian. Jerry's answer to this question may surprise you. His one piece of advice for the young comic was to write better jokes! Although this may seem like a condescending answer, he further elaborated on his response. He explained that the way to write better jokes is to write them every single day. When Jerry was a young comic, he bought a large wall calendar and hung it on his living room wall. Whenever he completed a writing session, he would mark a big red X on that day to signify his completion of the task. As the chain of X's began to grow, he felt motivated to continue adding to the chain. Eventually the chain got so long, he felt compelled to continue writing each day because he didn't want to break the chain. Over time, he refined his craft and eventually became one of the most successful comedians of the 20th century.

Anything you want to build confidence and mastery in will require a significant amount of time and effort to achieve. In the book *The One Thing* by Jay Papasan and Gary W. Keller, the authors explore how some of the best performers in the world achieved their success. One of the case studies profiled in the book is that of US Olympian swimmer Michael Phelps. Although Michael was diagnosed with ADHD at an early age, his ability to stay focused in the pool enabled him to become the most decorated Olympian of all time (22 medals in three Olympics). From age 14 through the Beijing Olympics in 2008, Phelps trained seven days per week, 365 days a year. He figured that by training on Sundays he got a 52-training-day advantage on his competition. Each day, he would spend up to six hours in the water. His coach Bill Bowman often cited his ability to channel his energy as being one of his greatest strengths.[7]

This point is further illustrated in Malcolm Gladwell's book *Outliers*. In the book, Malcom references a 1993 study that analyzed some of the best young violinists in the world to uncover how they were able to reach the pinnacle of the musical world. Malcolm Gladwell explained that on average, each student had reached at least 10,000 hours of "deliberate practice" before their 20th birthday.[8] What's deliberate practice? It's a special type of practice that's purposeful and systematic. While regular practice might involve mindless repetitions, deliberate practice requires focused attention and is conducted with the specific goal of improving performance.

What does this mean for us? Have we missed the boat if we didn't accumulate 10,000 hours of deliberate practice before age 20? Of course not. You need to consistently practice a skill for an extended period of time if you hope to become a master at it. Do you have a skill you want to improve upon? Do you want to improve your confidence in a certain area of your life? If so, you need to set aside time each day to deliberately practice the skill you want to improve upon. The resulting practice will improve your performance and build your confidence in performing the task.

Compete

Although the word "compete" may have many sports references, there are various other ways to compete. The word is derived from the Latin word "competere," which means *"to strive for."* In the context of confidence building, it means striving for excellence in everything you do. Whether it's the most minute detail or your biggest problem, applying the highest standards to every task you perform will fuel your desire to achieve excellence.

As an example, "compete" is a word that's part of the Seattle Seahawks creed. The Seahawks have been one of the most dominant NFL franchises over the past decade and their head coach, Pete Carrol, has instilled a culture of competition, accountability, and excellence into the organization. Pete will not accept anything less than the absolute best from his players and personnel. As a result, everyone's level of execution has increased substantially. From the players making better decisions on the field, to the coaches developing more effective game plans, to the front office making better personnel decisions, everyone is competing at a higher level. The distinction is that they're not competing against one another, they're competing against themselves and striving to be better every day. This creates a culture of self-improvement and everyone within the organization benefits.

The idea of competing with yourself to deliver superior results is also stressed in the book *Winning* by Jack Welch. During Jack's 20-year tenure at the helm of GE, the company experienced a 4000% growth in value and became one of the three largest companies on the planet. In the book, Jack highlights one of his first projects at GE. As a recent PhD chemical engineering graduate, Jack was tasked with delivering a presentation to his boss's boss about the small plastics business he was charged with running. Through relentless determination to compete with himself, Jack delivered a stellar presentation explaining improvements he made to existing business processes. Not only that, but he outlined how his small plastics business fit into the overall plastics market and provided strategies to help capture market share. Because Jack went above and beyond what was expected of him, he was able to distinguish himself from his peers and eventually became CEO of the entire company.

Make a commitment to strive for excellence in every situation you approach in life. If you're tasked with doing something at work, deliver more than what's expected of you. If you want to learn a new skill, double down and work twice as hard to improve yourself. If you continue this approach of over-delivering, you'll soon find you've become an expert in your field and that your confidence has skyrocketed.

Competency

This is the step of the confidence building process that has the most lasting impact. As you begin developing skills and expanding your knowledge, you'll naturally gain confidence. Over time, you'll become an expert in your field and may eventually evolve into the go-to resource for your company or organization. In the book *Outliers* by Malcolm Gladwell, Malcom explores how people develop mastery in a skill over time. As part of his analysis, he combed through various studies to uncover what factors determined whether someone was considered world-class in their field. What he discovered was quite intriguing. Regardless of what discipline (violinists, chess players, pianists, or master criminals, etc.), the distinguishing factor that determined whether an individual achieved world class status was the amount of deliberate practice they engaged in. These individuals had dedicated at least 10,000 hours of deliberate practice towards refining their craft. Although the 10,000-hour rule may not be an exact science, it's a metric that's useful to keep in mind. It will require extensive practice to gain confidence in your desired skill. Using 10,000 hours as your metric, if you worked eight hours per day five days per week, it would take you roughly five years to master a skill. Want to achieve mastery sooner? Be prepared to put in the time and effort to reach your goal.

It's also important to keep in mind that not all practice is created equal. In the book *Deep Work* by Cal Newport, Dr. Newport describes deep work as, *"Professional activities performed in a state of distraction-free concentration that push your cognitive ability to its limit. These actions deliver value, improve your skills, and are hard to replicate."* JK Rowling utilized deep work to write the last book of the *Harry Potter* series. To do this, she isolated herself in a five-star hotel near downtown Edinburgh for three weeks. Bill Gates developed his first software, Basic, in two months of feverish work. This software would eventually become the foundation of Microsoft. As of this writing (April 2018), Microsoft's market cap stands at 219 billion dollars!

These examples of deep work have become increasingly rare in our distraction filled society. With millions of tweets, posts, and comments bombarding us each day, it's no wonder people find it hard to concentrate. If you truly want to achieve mastery in your desired skill and build confidence in your ability, you'll need to isolate yourself from these distractions and allocate the proper time to immerse yourself within your craft.

Becoming a confident person

"Think positively and masterfully, with confidence and faith, and life becomes more secure, more fraught with action, richer in experience and achievement." – Eddie Rickenbacker

Now that we understand how confidence is developed, let's go over some strategies you can use to accelerate its growth and achieve the life of your dreams. In this section we'll discuss concepts related to using confident body language, explaining the power of positive self-talk, stepping out of your comfort zone, and various other confidence building strategies.

Using confident body language

While living and working in Washington DC, I loved attending networking events. On weekdays, I'd often go to meet ups to interact with other professionals living in the city. One of the most memorable events I attended was a meetup near DuPont Circle. This restaurant had opened its upstairs bar and there were professionals from all walks of life socializing with one another. As I made my way around the room, I struck up a conversation with a group of professionals near the bar. Although each person worked in a similar industry, the way they projected themselves was starkly different. The person to my left had a slouched posture, was frowning, and talked in a low and muddled tone. The lady to my right stood up straight, had her head held high, was smiling, and projected her voice with confidence and clarity.

Based on these two profiles, who do you think was more confident? Who was more successful? If you answered the latter individual, you wouldn't be alone. In a 2003 study led by Alexander Todorov, Professor Todorov suspected that, except for those people with hard-core political beliefs, the reasons we vote for particular candidates had less to do with politics and more to do with our perception of the candidate. In the study, over 1000 participants were asked to look at pictures of two individuals at a time to determine which person was more competent.

However, the participants didn't know they were actually looking at candidates from the senate and congressional races of 2000, 2002, and 2004. The results showed that the participants' pick for most competent had won their respective political races almost 73% of the time![14] In these instances, the candidate's body language, facial expression, and approachability were listed as some of the most common reasons for making their final decision. This astonishing revelation just goes to show how important having positive and confident body language is to achieving success in life. Projecting yourself to others in an inviting and confident manner can be the difference between landing that big pay day and finding yourself in the same position year in and year out.

In a study conducted by Amy Cuddy of Harvard University, Professor Cuddy examined two groups of students who were instructed to perform body poses. The first group was instructed to perform powerful poses, such as placing their hands at their sides and puffing out their chest, while the other group was instructed to perform weak poses, such as crossing their arms and slouching their shoulders. After two minutes of holding their pose, each participant was asked whether or not they wanted to gamble. Of the people in the power pose group, 86% opted to gamble while only 60% of the weak pose group did the same. Not only that, but when their saliva samples were tested, the group members who performed power poses had an 8% increase in testosterone levels and a 25% decrease in cortisol levels, a stress hormone, while the weak pose group had a 10% decrease in testosterone levels and a 15% increase in cortisol levels.[8] This means that the participants' brain chemistry actually changed as a result of how they projected themselves!

Now, I'm not suggesting you strike a Superman pose in the middle of your office. However, it's important to be cognizant of how you project yourself to others throughout the day. Incorporating a habit of striking a power pose before a difficult and stressful task has helped me perform noticeably better. What I periodically do throughout the day is stand with my hands on my hips and my chest out for about 30-60 seconds. After each session, I feel more relaxed and ready to tackle the day's challenges. I've provided a chart of power poses you can perform in the *Becoming a confident person* resource section of the book. I know it may seem unnatural, but try performing some of these exercises for yourself. I'm confident you'll see a positive change in your overall confidence and decision-making ability.

The power of positive self-talk

The power of words is something I've been conscious about my entire life. When I was younger, I'd often talk down to myself and feel as though I was less valuable than others. I'd tell myself that, *"I'm not as cool as other people," "I'm not good at sports,"* and *"I'm ugly and don't deserve to be loved."* These phrases rang around in my head like church bells on Sunday. However, as I grew up and discovered my strengths, I decided to change the way I talked to myself. From that day forward, I've adopted a more positive tone and now regularly engage in "positive self-talk." What's positive self-talk? It's the practice of talking to yourself in a positive way. Your mind is a powerful thing and if you're not careful, you'll start believing the negative things you tell yourself.

In a 2013 study led by a research team in the Netherlands, scientists observed anorexic women as they made their way through the lab. As the anorexic women performed various routines, the scientists noticed that patients would turn their shoulders to squeeze sideways through a door even when they had plenty of room.[22] They perceived themselves as overweight/fat and as a result contorted their body to fit through the door. To change a person's negative view of themselves, Dr. David Sarwer encourages his patients to stand in front of a mirror. During the exercise, he coaches his patient to use gentler and more neutral language to describe his/her body. For example, instead of saying, *"My abdomen is disgusting and grotesque,"* he'll prompt his patients to say, *"My abdomen is round; my abdomen is big; it's bigger than I'd like it to be."* By framing their dissatisfaction in this way, they're better able to make rational decisions about their bodies.[89]

Although a healthy dose of positive self-talk can help you overcome negative perceptions of yourself, not all positive self-talk is created equal. In a study conducted by Ethan Kross of the University of Michigan, Dr. Kross examined how the pronouns people use when talking to themselves can affect overall performance. In the study, two groups of participants were given five minutes to prepare an impromptu speech. The first group was instructed to use the pronoun "I" to describe themselves while the second group used "you." The results of the study showed that participants in the first group were more likely to say they experienced stress than those in the second group. Not only that, participants in the second group were more likely to offer themselves positive encouragement prior to delivering their speech. By using "you" instead of "I," the participants were able to mentally separate themselves from the stressful situation. Their ego was no longer being threatened and as a result they were able to approach the situation with a clearer mind.[91]

Have you been engaging in *negative* self-talk? Try replacing these negative phrases with ones that have a more positive and uplifting tone. Believe me when I say that the benefits you'll gain from this simple practice can be life-changing. In the *Becoming a confident person* section of the book, I've provided a list of the positive phrases I like to recite to start my day.

Stepping out of your comfort zone

Do you remember the first time you attempted to ride a bike? Although you may have felt excitement about trying something new, you probably felt equally terrified about falling and scraping your knees. I can recall many times in my life where I was fearful of new opportunities. However, many of these experiences turned into life defining moments that made me the person I am today.

Humans are hardwired to seek comfort and avoid risk and stress. In the days of early humans, if we ignored our natural fear and stress responses, we might have become lunch for a saber-tooth tiger or some other vicious predator. Although risk and stress can be detrimental if experienced consistently over time, they can also be great motivators. Imagine you have to deliver a big work presentation in 24 hours. You're unprepared and have struggled coming up with great content for your slides. In this situation, a little bit of stress could positively impact the situation by compelling you to frantically work on your slides. Once complete, you may practice your presentation in front of the mirror until you feel comfortable delivering it. After a few practice rounds, your stress will naturally subside and you'll begin to relax. Although your frantic reaction was a result of stress, it allowed you to rise to the challenge and complete your important task on time.

Similarly, stepping out of your comfort zone may feel awkward and stressful at first. Learning a new language, studying abroad in a new country, moving to a new city where you don't know anyone, and speaking in front of a group of 100 people are just some of the experiences that may initially cause discomfort. However, if you decide to take the leap of faith and absorb all the value they have to offer, you could find yourself becoming proficient in valuable skills that could serve you well in the future. Thomas Jefferson, one of the founding fathers and third president of the United States, was credited with saying, *"If you want something you've never had, you must be willing to do something you've never done."* I encourage you to heed his advice, and the next time a scary but promising opportunity arises, step out of your comfort zone and attack it head on.

Making more decisions

Imagine you're hanging out with friends and the topic of where to eat comes up. You start throwing around suggestions but no one seems willing to make the decision on which restaurant to go to. What's your reaction in this situation? Do you decide on the restaurant yourself or do you defer the responsibility to someone else? Although this decision may seem trivial, being the decision-maker can be difficult work. The fear of not pleasing everyone and the fear of rejection usually keeps people from making even trivial decisions. For you to gain confidence in your ability to lead others, you'll need to get over your fear of making decisions.

As far back as one million years ago, early humans needed the social approval of tribe members to survive throughout their life. Making decisions that upset members could result in being ousted from the tribe. If that happened, you were most likely going to die within a short time. As a result, we've evolved to avoid conflict and go with the flow as much as possible. This leads to us deferring decision-making to others in the group when the opportunity presents itself. Although this fear of rejection may have been legitimate in the past, we no longer live in a society where this fear is warranted. Even if you were to make a poor decision, you're most likely not going to die. We must learn to break through our fear of rejection and attack each decision we're faced with. Although being rejected may not kill you, it still hurts our ego and can leave us feeling down on ourselves. Also, the negative self-talk that often accompanies being rejected can erode your confidence and have you falling back in line with the crowd.

In a study conducted by Matthew Lieberman and his wife Naomi Eisenberger of UCLA, the professors examined subjects hooked up to brain scanners as they participated in a game played with two avatars. At the start of game, the participant and avatars passed the ball to one another. As the game progressed, the two avatars excluded the participant from the game and no longer passed them the ball. As a result, the pain centers of the participant's brain experienced a flurry of activity and expressed the emotional pain of being excluded. The observed brain patterns were almost identical to that of someone who just broke their leg![31]

The similarities between physical and emotional pain date back to pre-historic times. As highlighted in our previous example, being ostracized from the tribe would spell BIG trouble for you. In an article published by Dr. Alan Fogel, Professor of Psychology at the University of Utah, the professor explains, *"Our bodies decided to take the economy route and use a single neural system to detect and feel pain, regardless of whether it is emotional or physical."*[106] However, in order to overcome this hardwired fear, you must commit to making decisions regularly. Making more decisions will not only strengthen your decision-making muscle but will enable you to respond to challenging situations with a more objective approach.

Although making decisions in the long run will help build confidence and improve your decision-making ability, it's important to note that you should avoid making decisions purely based on emotion. Some of the most catastrophic decisions ever made were a result of people letting their emotions get the best of them. The decision to shoot your spouse when he/she has cheated on you, the decision to get behind the wheel of a car after you've been drinking, and the decision to continue your advances after your partner has said no are just some of the terrible decisions that can have life altering consequences for everyone involved. Adults make rational decisions based on rational judgement and as an adult you should conduct yourself accordingly.

If, however, you defer making the decision because you're afraid of what others might think, you'll be stuck with whatever decision is eventually made. This could be as simple as going to get Indian food when you hate spicy foods, or as big as being told to move to a location and job you hate. Decision-making is like a muscle; you need to consistently make decisions in order to get comfortable expressing yourself on a regular basis. As an exercise, try taking the lead the next time you're with your friends. If the subject of where to eat comes up, offer a suggestion and make the decision on where you plan to eat. This same logic can be applied the next time your friends want to plan a yearly trip or get together. When you're at the office, offer your opinion on a subject in a meeting, and if someone challenges your opinion, explain your rationale for the decision. Even making small changes can benefit your decision-making ability immensely.

Creating a positive support system

"Tis not enough to help the feeble up, but to support them after." – William Shakespeare

As you gain confidence in yourself, you'll notice that the confidence building process is not free from suffering. You'll fall from time to time and may feel as though it's impossible to get back up. Although you should accept the bulk of responsibility for moving forward, it's also important to develop positive and healthy relationships with others who support your goals and aspirations. In this section, we'll discuss various strategies you can use to create a positive support system.

It's OK to ask for help

Have you ever been afraid of asking someone for help? Over the past few years, I've discovered there are a few reasons why many people are reluctant to do so. As high performing Millennials, we tend to set high expectations for ourselves. We believe that if we set our mind to it, we can accomplish any goal we desire. Although this characteristic is a big reason for our success, it can lead to tunnel vision and us refusing the help of others when we face adversity. Many of us also have deep-rooted fears about what others might think if we ask for help. *"Will they think I'm stupid?"* and *"Will I be perceived as weak?"* are examples of some of the questions we ask ourselves. However, if you study the history of some of the most successful people in history, you realize that none of them made it to the top alone. Steve Jobs had Steve Wozniak, Larry Page had Sergey Brin, and Bill Gates had Paul Allen. All of these extremely successful individuals needed the help of others to achieve their audacious goals. If you find yourself stuck or need guidance in certain areas of your life, it's important to eliminate the artificial barriers keeping you from asking for help.

As mentioned previously, one of the most common reasons cited for not seeking help is the fear of rejection by others. The fear of being called stupid by classmates when asking a question in class, the fear of being taken advantage of in a competitive work environment, and the fear of being judged for being in a bad financial situation are all reasons for refusing the help of others. You'll need to overcome these hurdles if you hope to achieve any lasting change. According to a study conducted by Bruce J. Avolio and William L. Gardner of the University of Nebraska-Lincoln, individuals who were perceived as "authentic leaders" showed a remarkable willingness to be coached and seek out help.[20] Along with this, you'd be surprised with how likely people are to offer a helping hand to someone in need.

In a joint study performed by Stanford GSB professor Frank Flynn and Columbia PhD students, students on both Columbia and Stanford campuses were tasked with asking strangers for various favors. These tasks ranged from asking a stranger to borrow their cell phone to asking students to walk with them towards the campus gym. Before the experiment began, the participants were asked how likely the strangers were to comply with their request. At the end of the study, it was shown that participants had underestimated how likely people were to help them by 50%![1] Most people gladly obliged their request, and many students in the study were shocked with how often people reciprocated. Next time you find yourself in a situation where you feel as though you need help, don't be afraid to ask for it. I'm sure you'll be surprised with how positively people respond to your request.

Starting or joining a mastermind group

This is a concept I've wanted to incorporate into my life for quite some time. I didn't know about mastermind groups until my coach explained them to me last year. A mastermind group consists of likeminded individuals seeking to accomplish similar goals and aspirations. A common example would be an entrepreneurship mastermind group where like-minded entrepreneurs get together a few times per month to discuss their failures, successes, and goals for the future. These discussions often lead to finding innovative solutions to difficult problems because group members have diverse backgrounds and can view each problem from a different perspective. Also, the support provided by the group helps members overcome difficulties in their lives and renew motivation in their endeavors. Not only have I experienced a significant uptick in my performance since joining a mastermind group, but there are also an array scientific studies that explain just how powerful being part of a mastermind group can be.

In a meta-analysis performed by David Johnson, Roger Johnson, and Karl Smith of Minnesota University, the researchers analyzed 168 studies comparing cooperative learning, competitive learning, and individual learning. These studies included analysis of students performing lower-level cognitive tasks (e.g., knowledge acquisition and retention) and higher-level cognitive tasks (e.g., creative problem solving). It was shown that cooperative learning, similar to what you experience in a mastermind group, produced better overall results than competitive learning and individual learning. Not only that, but cooperative learning also had a positive impact on a host of other metrics such as self-esteem, confidence, and positive attitudes about learning.[2] Are you feeling stuck in a rut in your career, business, and/or life? A mastermind group may be just what you need to kick your performance into high gear.

In February 2018, I joined a mastermind group that comprises like-minded entrepreneurs looking to grow and develop their business. We have weekly calls where we discuss problems each group member is facing and provide feedback and discuss possible solutions. I've found my experience in this mastermind group EXTREMELY helpful, and I'm confident I wouldn't be where I am today without the insight and support provided by my awesome mastermind group members.

My mastermind group is organized by professional keynote speaker, coach, and entrepreneur Patrick Snow. He's sold upwards of one million copies of his books in five languages in 108 countries and has been instrumental in growing my speaking and coaching business this year. If you're looking to become a professional speaker, coach, best-selling author, and the like, I highly recommend looking into his coaching services. I've provided his contact information below:

http://patricksnow.com/contact-patrick-snow.php

Chapter 9
Continuing your education

◆

"Education is the passport to the future, for tomorrow belongs to those who prepare for it today." – Malcom X

For most people, learning stops after they graduate from high school, college, or graduate school. According to a Jenkins Group survey administered in 2003, 80% of households in the US did not read a book in 2002. Not only that, but 42% of all college graduates never read another book after college graduation![22] These staggering statistics show how little the average person focuses on continuing their education. In order to separate yourself from the pack, you'll need to dedicate yourself to continuous education. In this section, we'll go over some strategies you can utilize to expand your knowledge and horizons.

Sharpening the saw

Abe Lincoln once said that if he had six hours to chop down a tree, he would use four of them to sharpen his saw. President Lincoln understood the value of preparation and believed it a crucial part of succeeding in any endeavor. In the book, *The Seven Habits of Highly Effective People*, Stephen Covey talks about what it means to sharpen your mind so that you can prepare for the challenges you'll face in life. He describes the importance of consistently reading and educating oneself. Throughout his life, Stephen consistently read 10 pages of a good book daily, purchased courses, and attended conferences on subjects that developed valuable skills.

Through these experiences, he compounded his personal growth and he regularly encouraged his readers to do the same.

This concept of sharpening the saw of your mind has been utilized by many of the most successful individuals in the personal development industry. Jim Rohn, Ramit Sethi, Tim Ferriss, Brian Tracy, and many others have admitted to dedicating a large portion of their yearly income (often 10% or more) to educational materials and conferences that help them improve in various areas of their lives. In his book *Focal Point*, Brain Tracy explains the concept of increasing your value to increase your wealth over time.

In many of his seminars, he explains how he was able to increase his income by 1000% over the course of ten years. He reasons that since your wealth is directly correlated to the amount of value you provide to the marketplace, in order to increase your income by 1000% percent, you'll need to increase your value to the market place by 1000%. He suggests that instead of looking at this massive goal and becoming disheartened, try breaking it down into smaller pieces. Can you improve one-tenth of a percent each day? Of course, you can! That's such a minuscule amount. If you were to extrapolate this percentage out for 260 work days per year, you'd be improving yourself by 26% per year. Not a significant change but definitely noticeable. By continuing along this path for the next 10 years, you'll be able to improve by over 1000%! I've illustrated the math below.

*(1 + 1*0.26)^{10} = 10.08 ≈ 1008%!*

Use the methods highlighted in this section to focus on improving a small amount each and every day. Over the course of a ten-year period, you'll find that you're completely unrecognizable to the person you used to be.

Enrolling in Drive Time University

I, along with many Americans, commute to work each day. My commute is generally between 15-20 minutes each way depending on traffic. In the past, I used to listen to the radio and jam out to Justin Bieber's, Lady Gaga's, or Cardi B's latest tracks. However, after reading an article about how much I could learn from listening to educational material in my car, I decided to switch up my routine. According the US Census Bureau, American's spend an average of 51 minutes commuting to and from work each day. If you sum up all the commuting time over the course of a year it adds up to over 9.2 days ((51 minutes/60 minutes per hour * 261 work days)/24 hours in a day).[24] That means that the average American spends over one week of their life each year driving to and from work! I suggest that instead of dedicating that time to listening to the radio, you switch to listening to educational content.

This content could include educational podcasts, audiobooks, sales and leadership CDs, motivational content, industry specific content (i.e., software, sales, engineering, etc.), and any other form of content that helps develop valuable skills. Imagine if you resolved to listen to leadership training modules in your car for the next three years. At the end of those three years, you will have listened to over 663 hours of content! That's equivalent to over three months of full time work on the subject. Do you think you'd be a better leader after engaging with that much content on the subject? Of course you would. Not only that, but if you continue this routine over the course of your lifetime, you could be learning the equivalent of a PhD in any subject you desire.

One of the ways I've been able to read as many books as I have over the last two years is by listening to audiobooks via Audible. Audible is a subsidiary company of Amazon and is a platform that provides audible books to its customers. Along with listening to audiobooks during my commute, I listen to them while I work out, while I'm cooking meals for the week, and on my occasional morning jogs. I also jot down the best ideas from each book and share them with you via my blog and these books. By converting your downtime to educational time, you'll gain insight into whatever areas of your life you wish to improve upon and gain valuable skills in the process.

Allocating resources to continuous education

Bob Dylan's song, *"Time's they are a changin',"* beautifully describes how our environment changes over time. In order to ensure that you continue providing value to the marketplace, you'll need to constantly push yourself to learn and grow each day. As the famous author William S. Burroughs so eloquently put it, *"The moment you stop growing is the moment you start dying."* In many of his seminars, Brian Tracy recommends that people set aside at least 10% of their income each year for personal growth and development. He states that for every dollar you spend on your personal development, you can expect $30 to come back to you over your lifetime. That's a 3000% return! What other investments have such a high rate of return? Although it's not an exact science, many people, including myself, have followed Brian's advice and have experienced significant increases in our income and overall performance.

It's truly amazing how one idea or concept you pick up can change your life forever. Warren Buffet, one of the most successful investors in modern history, consistently references his decision to attend a public speaking seminar as one of the defining moments of his life. He's always been extremely bright, but as a young man he lacked the confidence and demeanor to speak in front of people. He often jokes about how the idea of giving a presentation in front of an audience was enough to cause him extreme anxiety. One day in his early twenties, he decided to attend a Dale Carnegie seminar to improve his public speaking skills. Although he was anxious at first, he overcame his fear and learned how to clearly and confidently express himself in front of an audience. This changed the course of his life and helped him land his first investors. The Dale Carnegie course cost him $100 to attend, and at the time of this writing he's worth over 80 billion dollars (February 2018). Although we can't attribute 100% of his success to the skills he developed in the Dale Carnegie course, even a fraction of a percent would amount to astronomical returns on his original investment.

In my own life, I've experienced the positive effects of dedicating my time, money, and energy towards continuing my education. One such instance came as a result of reading *The Compound Effect* by Darren Hardy for the first time. Although the e-book cost me $10 to purchase, the return on my investment has been many times that. One of the many ideas I picked up from the book was that daily deliberate action towards my goals can result in MASSIVE positive change over time. By applying this one idea into my life, I've been able to deliver over 20 presentations to thousands of individuals around the world, I've run a marathon, I've written two highly rated books, and am developing an in-depth course that will help my clients achieve their audacious goals. On top of all that, I'm in a happy and loving relationship with my beautiful girlfriend Melanie. I was able to achieve all this in just over two years. If you had asked me two years ago if this would be my reality in 2018, I would have probably laughed in your face. The mere fact that I invested the money and time necessary to read that book started me down a path that's led me to who I am today. What books, courses, and/or seminars have you invested in lately? In the *Continuing your education* section of the book, I've provided a list of the coursework and some of the books I've read since graduating from college. These materials have helped me improve in various areas of my life and the knowledge I've gained will stay with me for a lifetime.

Joining growth focused organizations

One of the best things you can do to grow as a person is to join a club/organization whose mission centers on developing its members. It's amazing the positive changes you can experience when you surround yourself with other like-minded individuals focused on personal development. One of the organizations I joined around two years ago is Toastmasters. Toastmasters is a nonprofit educational organization that operates clubs worldwide for the purpose of helping members improve their communication, public speaking, and leadership skills. As a result of engaging in Toastmasters curriculum and receiving feedback from other members, I've become a much better public speaker. I recently had the opportunity to speak to over 2300 students, faculty, and parents at the Kentucky Future Business Leaders of America Leadership conference! I've provided a highlight video of the speech here: (https://www.youtube.com/watch?v=-Od81Pfb78&t).

However, with so many different organizations and clubs out there, it can be hard to choose which one to get involved with. For a list of some of these organizations, check out the *Continuing your education* resources section at the end of this book.

Hiring a coach

About three years ago, I decided to hire a personal coach to help me achieve my yearly goals. Once every few weeks, I have a call with him to discuss my progress in various areas of my life. Many of these sessions involve us strategizing about how to best attack my over-arching goals for the year. As a result of our discussions, I've been able to write two books, run a marathon, give over 15 speeches (three completely in Spanish), and I'm on track to accomplish two other yearly financial goals I've set for myself. Coaching is a powerful tool you can use to achieve positive results in your life. The benefits of coaching are well documented and I'm a testament to that. A study conducted by PricewaterhouseCoopers (PwC) found that 70% of respondents saw improved work performance after working with a coach, and 80% stated they had improved self-confidence.[56]

The accountability provided by a coaching relationship is also extremely beneficial. Dr. Gail Matthews of the Dominican University in California performed a study that found that people who wrote down their goals, shared this information with a friend, and sent them weekly updates on their progress, were 33% more likely to accomplish their goals than participants who just formulated them.[57] I regularly talk about my goals with my coach and consistently send him updates on my progress. The accountability he's provided me has kept me on pace to achieve each of my yearly goals. Want to reach out to potential coaches? I found my coach via Thumbtack and have had great success with him thus far. Thumbtack is a business services platform where you can request services and receive bids from professionals looking to offer you their services. There are many reputable and effective coaches online who can help you reach your goals. Start a Thumbtack profile today and see what options are available to you.

Along with searching for a coach on Thumbtack, I also offer coaching services to individuals who are looking to improve their lives. Since 2016, I've had success coaching many individuals from diverse backgrounds and will work closely with you to help you accomplish your yearly goals. If you're interested in learning more about my services, I've provided a link to my coaching page below. Once you've reviewed the page, be sure to claim your 30-60-minute complimentary consultation!

www.raphaelcollazo.com/coaching

Taking on leadership roles in your community

One of the most rewarding things you can do with your time is to spend it giving back to your community. Along with making you feel good about yourself, taking on leadership roles within community organizations can teach you valuable lessons you can carry with you for the rest of your life. One of my first experiences with leadership came in the form of coordinating a community service event for my fraternity in college. As the co-Philanthropy coordinator, I was charged with setting up a yearly fundraiser to help raise money for a local Phoenix charity we were sponsoring. My responsibilities included reaching out to local restaurants to ask for food donations, meeting with local business owners to solicit monetary donations, and delivering presentations to different student organizations to help spread the word about the event. This role offered me the opportunity to gain experience in sales, public speaking, event planning, and fund-raising. Along with developing new and valuable skills, over 250 people participated in the event and we raised over $2000 for our sponsored charity. What roles can you take on in your community? Are there leadership positions at your church? How about other local organizations? Don't forget about some of the organizations discussed in the *Joining a growth focused organization* chapter. Most of these organizations offer yearly opportunities for their members to take on leadership roles.

Action Items

The 4C's of confidence

1) Commit to taking on a scary but promising opportunity within the next month.
   a. This could mean accepting a new job in a new city, joining a public speaking organization, asking out that person you've had a crush on, etc.
2) Pick a skill you want to improve upon and set aside one hour each week to improve that skill.
   a. Stick with your new routine for at least 6 months (preferably one year or more).
3) Pick one project you've been assigned at work/school and commit to over delivering on the requirements.
   a. Repeat this cycle with future projects.
4) Resolve to become an expert in your field within 5-7 years.
   a. Perform at least one action each day to bring you closer to your goal.

Becoming a confident person

5) Over the next month, commit to holding a high-power pose for 1-2 minutes each morning before work.
   a. For a list of high power poses, check out the *Becoming a confident person* resources section at the end of this book.
6) Over the next month, write out 3-5 positive phrases and commit to reciting 1-2 each day.
   a. Examples: *"I'm looking good," "I'm super smart," "I'm funny and everyone loves me,"* etc.
7) Remove the negative phrases you've been telling yourself from your vocabulary.

a. Examples: *"I'm so stupid," "No one likes me," "I'm fat and ugly,"* etc.

8) This month, try something you've been wanting to try but are fearful of.

   a. Examples: *"asking someone out on a date," "joining a public speaking club," "attending a dance class,"* etc.

9) Start making more decisions when you're around your friends.

10) Commit to sharing your opinion in a work meeting this week.

Creating a positive support system

11) This month, commit to asking for help on a project or task you've been struggling with.

12) Research mastermind groups in your area and write out a list of your top 3 choices.

   a. Select your top choice and commit to joining the group.

Continuing your education

13) Download an educational audio book and listen to it during your commute.

   a. Once finished, repeat this cycle.

14) Determine what one skill you most want to develop this year and purchase educational content (e.g., books, courses, and seminars) to help you develop this skill.

   a. Set aside at least 1 hour per week to engage with this content.

15) Look into joining at least one "growth focused" group by next month.

   a. For a list of organizations that fits this criterion, you can reference the *Continuing your education* resource section of the book.

For a printable PDF list of these action items, check out the link below:

https://bit.ly/2w2unMe

Beginning your journey

"Take action! An inch of movement will bring you closer to your goals than a mile of intention." – Dr. Steve Maraboli

Our time together has come to an end. Although this may be the end of the book, it's only the beginning of your journey. Throughout this book you've learned strategies that, if implemented, will serve you well for the rest of your life. However, now the hard part begins. Commit to dedicating the proper time and effort to making your dreams a reality. The great Mohandas Gandhi often said, *"Action expresses priorities."* Only through massive action can you take the difficult but necessary steps towards making significant positive changes in your life. Don't be discouraged if implementing these changes is difficult at first. I'm confident that with this book as your guide, you can accomplish any goal you set your mind to.

This is an ever-evolving text, and if you have some insights you feel would benefit our readers, please reach out and share. Also, as a FREE gift to you, I'd like to offer you a chapter from the next book of the Millennial Playbook series. In the book, we'll focus on topics related to professional development for Millennials. To download your FREE chapter, check out the link provided here: https://bit.ly/2CX2Kes

Whether you need words of encouragement or just want to share your success stories, please reach out to me via email. I'd love to hear from you and am excited for your future successes!

****

<u>Note from the Author:</u> Reviews are gold to authors! If you've enjoyed this book, would you consider rating and reviewing it at https://amzn.to/2QArnjw?

****

Booking Raphael Collazo to speak at your next event!

When it comes to choosing a professional speaker for your next event, you'll find no one more respected or successful—no one who will leave your audience or colleagues more empowered—than Raphael Collazo, one of the most gifted speakers of our generation. Since 2014, Raphael has delivered speeches to thousands of high school students, university students, and professionals across America and abroad.

Whether your audience is 10 or 10,000, in North America or abroad, Raphael Collazo can deliver a customized message of inspiration for your meeting or conference. Raphael understands your audience does not want to be "lectured," but is rather interested in hearing stories of inspiration, achievement, and real-life people reaching their goals.

As a result, Raphael Collazo's speaking philosophy is to humor, entertain, and inspire your audience with passion and stories proven to help people achieve extraordinary results. If you're looking for a memorable speaker who will leave your audience wanting more, book Raphael Collazo today! To see a highlight video of Raphael Collazo and find out whether he's available for your next event, visit his website at the address below. Then contact him by phone or via email to schedule a complimentary pre-speech phone interview:

www.raphaelcollazo.com/speaking
recollaz@gmail.com
Mobile: 520-456-4679

Hiring Raphael Collazo as your coach!

Do you feel as though you're falling behind in certain areas of your life? Do you have big dreams and aspirations but lack the guidance and accountability to get you there? Do you feel as though you're falling short of reaching your full potential? If you answered yes to any of these questions, then hiring a coach may be a great option for you! The improvements you can experience working with a coach are well documented and were a focal point of this book.

Raphael Collazo is a Millennial coach, professional keynote speaker, and author who has sold thousands of books and spoken to thousands of students and professionals across the United States and abroad. He's helped many Millennials achieve their goals through his unique coaching style. His honest yet supportive approach makes for a positive learning experience and supports the overall development of his clients. He'll also work with you to design a custom coaching plan that fits your schedule and unique needs while holding you accountable to execute it.

Through his one-on-one coaching calls, unlimited email and text access, and his proprietary coaching content, you'll reach your goals faster than you ever thought possible! For more information, visit the website provided below and then text him your name, time zone, and the best time to redeem your 30-60 minute, no-obligation coaching consultation by phone or Skype.

www.raphaelcollazo.com/coaching
recollaz@gmail.com
Mobile: 520-456-4679

Resources

Welcome to the resource section of this book. In this section, I've provided some helpful resources related to the six principles discussed in this book. I hope you find these useful, and I'd love to get your feedback on them. Also, be sure to like, share, and follow us on social media and stop by the blog and YouTube channel to check out more awesome free content:

Website: https://www.raphaelcollazo.com
Blog: http://thestrongprofessional.com/
Facebook: https://www.facebook.com/thestrongprofessional/
YouTube: https://www.youtube.com/channel/UCjhfTMKK7prM_zH0wuJyuAQ
LinkedIn: https://www.linkedin.com/in/raphaelcollazo/
Pinterest: https://www.pinterest.com/recollaz/
Twitter: https://twitter.com/thestrongprof

Developing a winning psychology

As we discussed in this chapter, developing a winning psychology is crucial if you ever hope to reach your full potential. Below I've outlined an exercise I used to discover my "why" and explain how you can use it to do the same.

The 7 layers of depth exercise

To come up with my "WHY," I tried out an exercise Dean Graziosi calls *"the 7 layers of depth."* Start by asking yourself "WHY" you do what you do and write down the answer on a piece of paper. Once you've written out your answer, ask yourself the same question again. Continue this exercise until you've answered the question seven times. It's pretty amazing what answers you come up with if you continue to whittle down your responses. I know I was shocked by the end of the exercise. Try it out for yourself and see what answers you come up with. I've provided a picture of my responses below:

Why?	Response
Why did you write this book Raphael?	Because I wanted to share strategies that will help millions of Millennials around the world develop a postive mindset and live happy and fulfilling lives.
Why did you want to help Millions of Millennials?	Because I feel that our generation has a lot to contribute and helping others achieve their goals makes me feel amazing.
Why does it feel amazing to help others?	Because it helps satisfy my human need to connect with others and affords me the opportunity to build a successful business based on solid values.
Why is it important to build a successful business based off solid values?	Because I want to provide stability for my family and leave a legacy they would be proud of.
Why is it important to provide stability and leave a legacy for your family?	Because I know how much my family had to sacrifice in order to put me in a position to do so.
Why does your family's sacrifices matter to you?	Because I don't want my family to have to deal with financial struggles.
Why don't you want your family to deal with financial struggles?	Because I want myself and my family to have choices and have the freedom to do what we love each day.

Books on developing a winning psychology:

The Compound Effect by Darren Hardy

This was one of the books that changed the way I viewed personal development. In the book, success coach Darren Hardy talks about how small positive daily actions performed over an extended period of time can add up to BIG results. He uses various examples to drive home the point and recommends different routines to get you started on your personal development journey. It's one of my favorites, and it's 100% worth the read. I've provided a link to the book below:

https://www.amazon.com/Compound-Effect-Darren-Hardy-ebook/dp/B005P1YCNK/ref=sr_1_1?ie=UTF8&qid=1497002580&sr=8-1&keywords=the+compound+effect

Be Obsessed or Be Average by Grant Cardone

Has anyone ever called you "obsessed" with what you're doing? Well, according to Grant Cardone, you may be on the right track. In the book, Grant discusses how giving into your obsessions is the only way to succeed in this ultra-competitive world. He talks about some of the opposition you'll face from strangers and the ones you love and how to fight through mediocrity to achieve greatness. This book was extremely insightful and changed my perspective on how I view what I do day to day. I've provided a link to the book below:

https://www.amazon.com/Be-Obsessed-Average-Grant-Cardone-ebook/dp/B016VRFTR4/ref=sr_1_1?ie=UTF8&qid=1497002689&sr=8-1&keywords=be+obsessed+or+be+average

The Slight Edge by Jeff Olsen

Have you ever wondered how some people are able to achieve seemingly impossible feats almost effortlessly? According to Jeff Olsen, there's a science behind it. In the book, you'll learn how taking daily actions towards your goals will add up to big results over time. You'll also gain insight into the importance of routines when seeking to accomplish big goals. I found the book extremely helpful and loved the actionable content provided at the end of each chapter. I've provided the link to the book below:

https://www.amazon.com/Slight-Edge-Turning-Disciplines-Happiness/dp/1626340463/ref=sr_1_1?s=books&ie=UTF8&qid=1520216004&sr=1-1&keywords=the+slight+edge

Achieving happiness

Learning how to achieve happiness in life will pay dividends for you in the future. As discussed previously, the mind plays a pivotal role in how we interact with our environment. In this section,

I'll provide various strategies you can use to shape your mind into one that's open to receiving and projecting happiness towards others.

Using social comparison for good

Making social comparisons with an empathetic perspective can have lasting effects on your mood and sense of wellbeing. We must seek to understand another person's situation before we can hope to relate to them effectively. Below, I've provided various questions you can ask yourself prior to making a social comparison:

Upward comparison

- [ ] *What are some of the qualities I admire about this person?*

- [ ] *What are some of the qualities I dislike about this person?*

- [ ] *How does this person feel about their current situation?*

- [ ] *Are they facing any challenges/struggles that I'm unaware of?*

- [ ] *How am I similar to this person?*

    - o *List various positive qualities.*

- [ ] *What can I do to emulate the positive qualities of this individual?*

Downward comparison

- [ ] *What are some of the struggles they're experiencing at the moment?*

- [ ] *How did they get into their current situation?*

- [ ] *How would I feel if I was in a similar position?*

□   *How am I similar to this person?*

    o   *List various positive qualities.*

□   *What could I do to help their current situation?*

By asking yourself these questions prior to making any comparison, you'll be better able to empathize with the individual and capitalize on the benefits of social comparison.

Laughter is the best medicine

Ready for some ideas on how to increase the frequency of laughter throughout the week? Below I've provided a few of my favorite activities and some that were recommended to me by my clients. I hope you enjoy:

1) Share something silly about yourself with a friend or family member.

We all have funny stories that have happened to us in the past. Why not share them with the ones you love? I used this technique on a few occasions to get myself and my girlfriend to laugh. My past misfortunes are SOOO amusing to her, lol.

2) Watch a funny TV show with someone you love.

My girlfriend loves *The Office,* and every once and while I like to sit back and relax with her as we watch a few episodes together. Steve Carrell kills me every time.

3) Support funny people by going to a comedy show.

I've been to a few comedy shows throughout my life, and I have to say it's one of my favorite things to do. There are so many talented and funny comedians out there who know how to make people laugh. The next time a comedian comes to town, grab some tickets for you and your loved one to enjoy the show.

4) Play pretend

Although this one may seem odd to some of you, the benefits of playing pretend are actually backed by science. Katherine Puckett, national director of Mind-Body Medicine at the Cancer Treatment Centers of America, leads Laughter Club for patients, family, and staff. Even when facing serious illness, she urges members to give themselves "permission to play," which will lighten the mood and, hopefully, cue the laughs. Various studies have also shown how a positive mood helps people cope with serious illnesses. One particular study went as far as saying, *"It's apparent that optimism is a mental attitude that heavily influences physical and mental health."*[93]

Try out some of these techniques for yourself and see what a difference it makes. If you have any other techniques you use to help you laugh more throughout the day, I'd love to hear from you!

Learn to love yourself

Below I've provided a Trail Based Cognitive Therapy worksheet you can use to eliminate some of your limiting beliefs and implement new positive ones:

Positive Belief Record

Old (self-critical) belief:____

New (positive) belief:____

Evidence that supports the new belief (or isn't entirely consistent with the old belief):
(e.g. an experience you have, something someone says to you, or anything else that supports the new belief)

1.____

2.____

3.____

4.____

5.____

6.____

7.____

8.____

9.____

10.____

creative commons http://psychologytools.com

Determining your values

In this section, you created a list of events in your life that made you feel proud, extremely fulfilled, and happy. You'll now want to identify the values that line up with these experiences. Below I've listed some of the most common values shared by people around the world. Your perfect value may not be listed here, so be sure to explore other values that may describe you better:

Authenticity, Achievement, Adventure, Authority, Autonomy, Balance, Beauty, Boldness, Compassion, Challenge, Citizenship, Community, Competency, Contribution, Creativity, Curiosity, Determination, Fairness, Faith, Fame, Friendships, Fun, Growth, Happiness, Honesty, Humor, Influence, Inner Harmony, Justice, Kindness, Knowledge, Leadership, Learning, Love, Loyalty, Meaningful Work, Openness, Optimism, Peace, Pleasure, Poise, Popularity, Recognition, Religion, Reputation, Respect, Responsibility, Security, Self-Respect, Service, Spirituality, Stability, Success, Status, Trustworthiness, Wealth, Wisdom

My top five values are *Integrity, Excellence, Impact, Family,* and *Leadership*. I'd love to hear what your values are!

Books on achieving happiness:

The Book of Joy by Dalai Lama & Archbishop Desmond Tutu

Have you ever wondered what it means to be truly happy? Lucky for us, the Dalai Lama and Archbishop Desmond Tutu have dedicated a large portion of their lives to answer this very question. In the book, the two men discuss their life journeys and what it means to be truly happy. I found the content of this book extremely insightful. I especially liked the section that discussed taking responsibility for how you feel and how to adopt a positive mindset. Anyone can benefit from the ideas shared by these two holy men and I feel that this book should be required reading for all. I've provided a link to the book below:

https://www.amazon.com/Book-Joy-Lasting-Happiness-Changing/dp/B01IQ15JA0/ref=sr_1_1?ie=UTF8&qid=152042562 2&sr=8-1&keywords=the+book+of+joy

The Subtle Art of Not Giving a F*ck by Mark Manson

As the author of his own popular blog, Mark Manson is known for not pulling any punches when it comes to expressing his opinions. Although this book can be harsh at times, the ideas and concepts discussed may be just the reality check you need to take control of your emotions, passions, and life. In the book, you'll learn how to overcome the negative voices in your head and how to not care about what others think of you. Using these techniques, you can begin to focus on what's really important in life and start making a positive impact on others. I highly recommend the book and have provided the link below:

https://www.amazon.com/Subtle-Art-Not-Giving-Counterintuitive/dp/0062457713

You are a Badass by Jen Sincero

This is one of my girlfriend's favorite self-help books. In her book, Jen Sincero explores many of the limiting beliefs people experience throughout their lives and provides unique insight on how to battle these thoughts to reach your full potential. I loved how Jen was able to deliver an important and poignant message in a playful and inspiring way. I highly recommend the book and have provided the link below:

https://www.amazon.com/You-Are-Badass-Doubting-Greatness-ebook/dp/B00B3M3VWS

Developing positive relationships

One of the most fulfilling parts of life is establishing positive and long-lasting relationships with your family and friends. In this section, we discussed how to classify your current influences, identify positive influences, and add more of these individuals into your life. Below, I've elaborated on some of the strategies you can use to establish positive relationships with "expanded" associations.

Expanded associations

Although these strategies have worked for me and others in the past, I cannot 100% guarantee their success in every situation. With that being said, if utilized effectively, these strategies can significantly increase your chances of developing life changing relationships:

1. Start a conversation with the individual at an event.

    a. If it's a recurring meeting, follow up with them and take an interest in their life.

2. Offer to help them out with something they've been working on.

    a. Example: Offer to evaluate their speech at a Toastmasters meeting, offer to come in and speak to their students, offer to volunteer at a community event they've organized, etc.

3. Ask them about what they did when they were your age to set themselves up for success.

    a. Once they give you their advice… ACT ON IT! You'll eventually want to follow up and share your results.

4. Ask to interview them for a local project/book you're working on.

5. Offer to buy a cup of coffee and ask for 10 minutes of their time.

   a. This is the least effective way of approaching an "expanded" relationship initially. Nurture the relationship before making this offer.

By continually practicing these techniques, you'll slowly begin developing relationships with more expanded associations. After a few years, you may even be able to call them close friends!

Books on developing positive relationships:

The 5 Love Languages by Dr. Gary Chapman

Although I don't usually read books on "romance," the insights I've gained from this book have already helped improve my relationship with my girlfriend. In the book, Dr. Gary Chapman highlights the five ways people like to give and receive love from their significant other. By understanding how your significant other best receives love, you can greatly increase the satisfaction you each experience within your relationship. My girlfriend's love languages are *"Quality Time"* and *"Words of Affirmation,"* and I now express love in these ways. As a result, I've been able to love her in a way that makes her feel special and wanted. I highly recommend this book for anyone looking to improve their relationship with their significant other. I've provided a link to the book below:

https://www.amazon.com/Love-Languages-Secret-that-Lasts/dp/080241270X

Give and Take by Adam Grant

Have you ever wondered what makes some people so much more effective than others? Do you agree with the statement *"nice guys finish last"*? According to Adam Grant, you may want to rethink that statement. In the book, Adam Grant shares insights on people's predisposition to give and take in interactions. From these tendencies, Adam classified people into one of three categories ("Giver," "Taker," and "Matcher") and analyzed how effective they were in certain situations. As a "Giver," I found the book's insights extremely intriguing, and I'll be utilizing some of the strategies recommended by Adam. I highly recommend the book and have provided the link below:

https://www.amazon.com/Give-Take-Helping-Others-Success/dp/0143124986

Developing positive habits

One of the most effective ways to increase your likelihood of long term success is to develop positive habits. The Orpah's, Richard Branson's, and Michael Jordan's of the world all developed positive habits over time. However, one of the biggest challenges you'll face along the way is holding yourself accountable to meet these expectations. In the resources below, I'll discuss strategies I've used in the past to hold myself accountable to establishing worthwhile habits.

Holding yourself accountable

Striving towards audacious goals can be tough work. Before utilizing the following strategies and seeking the help of a coach, I'd often fall short of reaching my goals and get disheartened as a result. Below, I've provided these useful strategies and go over how you can become more accountable to yourself and others.

Using www.stickk.com

Have you ever heard of http://www.stickk.com/? It's a website I used to incentivize myself to write this book and get my first five coaching clients. According to various scientific studies, human beings are more likely to react to avoid loss than to seek gains. In a 1979 paper published by Nobel Laureate Daniel Kahneman and his colleague Amos Tversky, the two scientists discovered that "loss aversion" plays a key role in how we make decisions.[107] What's "loss aversion"? In economics and decision theory, loss aversion refers to people's tendency to prefer avoiding losses to acquiring equivalent gains: *It's better to not lose $5 than to find $5.*

Using this logic, the founders of "stickK" created a website where users set goals, assign a monetary wager for reaching that goal, and choose a form of "punishment" if they fail. If you fail to meet your objective in the allotted time, your accountability partner(s) will donate your wager to an "anti-charity." An anti-charity is a charity or organization you'd hate to support or give money to. For example, if you hate guns, a good candidate for an anti-charity would be the NRA or other gun related groups. If you're a stanch republican, a good candidate may be the Democratic National Convention. You get the idea. To start, come up with a goal you want to accomplish and then invite friends to hold you accountable. Next, you'll choose an anti-charity and assign a monetary wager to donate to if you fail to accomplish your goal. Make sure this amount is significant enough to elicit a negative response if you were to lose. Once complete, you'll communicate with your friends, instructing them to execute the transaction if you fail to reach your goal by the deadline. Make sure your accountability buddy has the stomach to overlook your pleas and whines if you fail to reach your goal by the deadline. Now that you have everything set up, start working towards your desired outcome. With your anti-charity in the back of your mind, you'll be much more likely to take the necessary steps towards achieving your goal.

Sharing on social media

When I decided to establish a morning writing routine, I made myself publicly accountable to others by sharing my desired habit via my blog and social media. By doing this, I showed my family, friends, and contacts that I was serious about implementing the habit and that I needed to be held accountable. Although I struggled initially, the public accountability added fuel to my inner fire and pushed me to get out of bed early each morning. As a result, I was able to establish a writing routine and have since written two books and started a third. It's an extremely valuable exercise that I highly recommend.

Finding a coach

This was the single most effective option that kept me accountable to reaching my goals. Every other week, I would have a one-hour coaching call to discuss the progress I had made towards my goals. Along with that, if I had fallen short of expectations, I'd strategize with my coach to see what I could improve upon over the next two weeks to get me back on track. I've had two coaches over the last 2 ½ years, and each specializes in different areas of development. I found my first coach Scott on www.Thumbtack.com. As discussed in a prior chapter, Thumbtack is an online marketplace where professionals sell their services. There are many reputable coaching professionals on the site and I highly recommend you browse to see if you find a coach whose expertise lines up with your desired area of improvement.

Books on developing positive habits:

The Power of Habit by Charles Duhigg

Have you ever wanted to change a bad habit or implement a good one? In this book, Charles Duhigg gives you a blueprint for doing just that. This is an awesome book with a substantial number of examples of how good habits are formed and bad habits are broken. I've used the techniques discussed in this book to implement new, beneficial habits into my own life and eliminate some of my bad habits. This is an unbelievable book with life-changing content and I highly recommend it. I've provided the link to the book below:

https://www.amazon.com/Power-Habit-What-Life-Business-ebook/dp/B0055PGUYU/ref=sr_1_1?ie=UTF8&qid=1497002273&sr=8-1&keywords=the+power+of+habit

The 7 Habits of Highly Effective People by Stephen Covey

This timeless classic has sold more than 25 million copies since its publication in 1989. In the book, Stephen Covey intricately details the seven habits the most effective people in the world possess and how you can implement these habits into your own life. I found the book extremely insightful and loved the simple truths he shared in this book. It was easy to digest and had actionable content readers can use to effectively implement these strategies into their own life. I highly recommend it and have provided the link to the book below:
https://www.amazon.com/Habits-Highly-Effective-People-Powerful/dp/0743269519

Triggers by Marshall Goldsmith

Have you ever wondered why bad habits keep rearing their ugly head no matter how hard you try to get rid of them? In this book, Dr. Goldsmith analyzes how triggers in our environment drive the actions we perform every day. He shares insights on how to make positive behavioral changes in your life and maintain them long-term. This was a very eye-opening book for me and I highly recommend it. I've provided a link to the book below:

https://www.amazon.com/Triggers-Creating-Behavior-Becoming-Person/dp/B00UKE4ZZ2/ref=sr_1_4?s=books&ie=UTF8&qid=15 20511624&sr=1-4&keywords=triggers

Creating S.M.A.R.T. goals

In this chapter, you discovered the benefits of writing out your S.M.A.R.T. goals. This is a practice that can pay HUGE dividends for you over the course of your life. However, prior to writing out your goals, you'll need to define your values. This will ensure your goals line up with your beliefs and lead down a path towards long-term fulfillment. In the resources below, I've outlined my optimal life and how I use this as my baseline to craft my yearly S.M.A.R.T. goals.

Outlining your optimal lifestyle

On Sunday, January 20, 2018, I decided to write out my optimal lifestyle. Below, I've provided my answers to the various questions highlighted in the section:

1) *Where do you live?*

I live in a larger city with a warm climate year-round. My house has four bedrooms, three bathrooms with hardwood floors, high ceilings, and a large open kitchen. I have my own private gym on site and have an outdoor swimming pool where I can swim laps twice per week.

2) *Do you have a spouse?*

I have a loving and supportive spouse who challenges me to achieve my goals. We bring out the best in each other and I love her unconditionality. She's also engaged in the community and supports causes she's passionate about.

3) *Do you have children?*

My spouse and I have two to three children, one of which is adopted. We love them unconditionality while supporting and cultivating their unique talents. They are happy, healthy, and loving children who are passionate about helping others.

4) *What's your job/career?*

I'm an author, speaker, and entrepreneur who runs various successful companies. I travel a few times per month and enjoy meeting new people from all over the world. I challenge my employees every day to be the best version of themselves and provide extreme value to my customers. My companies are heavily involved in the community and make a positive impact on the lives of others.

5) *What's your financial situation look like?*

I make between \$80,000-\$100,000 in net profit each month and reinvest 40% into the business. I allocate 30% of the funds to other investments such as real estate and stocks and use 15% for living expenses. The left over 15% of the income will go towards establishing a foundation to support causes I'm passionate about.

6) *What are your hobbies?*

My hobbies include writing, reading, playing basketball, and taking trips to other countries around the world. I dedicate between eight to ten hours per week to these activities.

7) *How many days off do you have per year?*

Although I love my work, I understand the value of taking time to recharge and refuel. Each week, Sunday will be my day to go completely off the grid. On top of that, I set aside time to take a weekend trip each quarter, a weeklong trip twice a year, and a two-week trip once per year.

8) *How many hours do you dedicate to work, family, friends, and faith?*

I dedicate 50-60 per week to working on my businesses and myself. Another 20 hours will be dedicated to family activities and engagements while I use 10 hours per week to focus on personal development and charitable organizations.

9) *What do the various people in your life think about you?*

a) My family loves me unconditionally and views me as a loving and caring person. They know I'll always be there for them and they can rely on me. They often seek my advice and view me as a competent person both personally and professionally.

b) My friends view me as a loving, caring, and supportive person. They know I want the best for them and will often seek my advice during difficult life decisions. We get together a few times each year and enjoy each other's company.

c) My colleagues love and respect me. They know I have their best interest in mind and can expect me to be honest and sincere with them. They appreciate me challenging them and they love the work they do each day.

10) What charities and/or causes do you regularly support?

I've created a foundation that helps support under represented youths who are passionate about engineering, entrepreneurship, and business. Each year we award over $100,000 in scholarships to deserving students across the nation and provide mentorship and other resources to help these students achieve their goals.

Books on creating S.M.A.R.T. goals:

The School of Greatness by Lewis Howes

Have you ever wanted to achieve greatness in a particular area of your life? In this book, Lewis Howes explains how some of the most successful people on the planet were able to achieve their success. I found his story extremely inspiring, and I value much of the advice he shares in the book. I especially liked his advice on goal setting and would highly recommend the book to others. I've provided a link to the book below:

https://www.amazon.com/School-Greatness-Real-World-Living-Leaving/dp/1522614346

Write It Down, Make It Happen by Henriette Anne Klauser

Do you have big dreams and audacious goals that seem out of reach? Do you feel like you're meant for something bigger but don't know how to get there? Well, writing down your goals and aspirations may get you closer to achieving them. In this book, Dr. Klauser explains how the simple act of writing down your goals, dreams, and aspirations increases the likelihood of you actually achieving them. I found the insights in this book extremely valuable and I highly recommend it. I've provided a link to the book below:

https://www.amazon.com/Write-Down-Make-Happen-Knowing/dp/0684850028/ref=tmm_pap_swatch_0?_encoding=UTF8&qid=1525051307&sr=8-1

Bookending your days

The concept of bookending my days has paid huge dividends for me over the past two years. Since implementing my morning routine in early 2016, I've been able to complete two books (writing my third), achieve a leaner physique, deliver over 20 speeches to thousands of people across the country, contribute to two successful software rollouts, and now I'm able to approach each day's challenges with a clear mind and cool demeanor. In this section, I'll outline the morning exercise regimen I used for a few months in 2017.

Weekly morning exercise routine

In early May 2016, I began incorporating a light exercise regimen into my morning routine. It really doesn't take much to get the benefits of morning exercise. My session usually lasts for between five to fifteen minutes and I feel great afterwards. Below, I've provided a weekly workout routine that I used from June 2017-September 2017. Try it out for yourself, and I bet you'll start to see some benefits too.

Monday: (3 sets)
100 jumping jacks
25 push ups
30 seconds of air boxing
30 leg lifts

Tuesday: (3 sets)
100 jumping jacks
25 couch dips
12 lunges (each leg)
50 bicycle kicks

Wednesday: (3 sets)
100 jumping jacks
25 squats
20 elevated push ups
30 seconds butterfly kicks

Thursday: (3 sets)
100 jumping jacks
Wall sits (45 seconds)
Planks (45 seconds)
12 step ups (each leg)

Friday: (3 sets)
100 jumping jacks
25 push ups
30 sit ups
25 couch dips

You can use different variations of this workout routine in future sessions. By utilizing these exercises, you'll be well on your way to achieving a healthy lifestyle.

Books on bookending your days:

The Miracle Morning by Hal Ellrod

The majority of the most successful people in the world have a scripted morning routine. In the book, Hal Ellrod describes how he rose from a very dark time in his life to being one of the top sales professionals in his industry by utilizing a morning routine. I love this book because Hal gives you step by step instructions on what routines to incorporate into your mornings and the benefits associated with each routine. I highly recommend this book for anyone looking to establish a more concrete morning ritual. I've provided a link to the book below:

https://www.amazon.com/s/ref=nb_sb_noss_2?url=search-alias%3Daps&field-keywords=the+miracle+morning

Sleep Smarter by Shawn Stevenson

Sleep has become a controversial topic among Millennials. Many believe that in order to achieve success in life they have to "burn the midnight oil" and be an "early riser." Although it's important to work hard for what you want, it's shortsighted to overlook the positive impact restful sleep can have on overall wellbeing. In the book, Shawn Stevenson talks about his early health struggles and how he was able to overcome them utilizing the healing power of sleep. I found the advice in this book phenomenal and use many of the strategies suggested in my own life. I highly recommend it and have provided the link below:

https://www.amazon.com/Sleep-Smarter-Essential-Strategies-Success-ebook/dp/B019G14UQI

Becoming a confident person

In the *Becoming a confident person* section of the book, we highlighted various strategies you could use to improve your overall confidence. Although it can take time to develop confidence, there are ways to expedite the process. Below, I elaborate on a few strategies that will help you do just that.

Using confident body language

In this section, we discussed how projecting confident body language can positively impact your overall confidence. Below, I've provided a chart created by Harvard Professor Amy Cuddy which illustrates various *High Power* and *Low Power* poses. Try a few poses for yourself and see what a difference they make in your overall confidence.

The power of positive self-talk

Each morning, I like to recite a few positive phrases to start my day off right. These messages highlight various aspects of my life and have a positive and uplifting tone. Below, I've provided a few of my favorites:

1) *Your life is meaningful and your purpose is clear.*

2) *You're a gifted writer/speaker and your words will touch millions of lives around the world.*

3) *You contribute to your organization and are a valuable asset to the team.*

4) *Your failures will become your defining moments.*

5) *I'm a loving and caring person who wants to leave his mark on the world.*

6)   I love myself and am excited for the day ahead.

7)   Whatever I believe, I can achieve.

Books on becoming a more confident person:

Presence by Amy Cuddy

How does the way you project yourself affect your self-confidence? That was the question Amy Cuddy sought to answer when she delivered her TedTalk on *The Power of Presence* in 2012. If you haven't already, I highly recommend watching her speech. It's extremely informative, inspiring, and shows how significant a role presence plays in human interaction. I've provided the link here: (https://www.ted.com/talks/amy_cuddy_your_body_language_shapes_who_you_are). In her book *Presence*, Amy showcases her research on how presence effects a person's overall confidence and wellbeing. I found the topics discussed in this book extremely fascinating, and I took away many strategies that I utilize today to calm my nerves before big meetings. I've provided the link below:

https://www.amazon.com/Presence-Bringing-Boldest-Biggest-Challenges-ebook/dp/B00U6DNZK8/ref=sr_1_3?s=digital-text&ie=UTF8&qid=1521805001&sr=1-3&keywords=presence

Grit by Angela Duckworth

This is one of my favorite books of 2017. In the book, professor Duckworth highlights her research into what makes some people achieve more than others. After years of study the answer she came up with was *grit*. Throughout the book she goes through examples of how to develop a positive mindset and fight through adversity to achieve your goals. As someone who recently faced adversity in my professional and personal life, I found this book to be a great guide on how to keep the faith in times of struggle. I highly recommend the book and have provided the link below:

https://www.amazon.com/Grit-Passion-Perseverance-Angela-Duckworth-ebook/dp/B010MH9V3W/ref=sr_1_1?s=digital-text&ie=UTF8&qid=1521805216&sr=1-1&keywords=Grit

The Confidence Code by Katty Kay and Claire Shipman

It's hard being a woman in business. There are conflicting expectations on how a woman should act in the workplace, and the external social pressures of starting a family and fulfilling family obligations can be overwhelming. In this ever more demanding world, women need to have the confidence to attack life head on and accept its many challenges. In this book, Katty and Claire interview some super achieving women to uncover how they developed and maintained their confidence over time. They also highlight various scientific studies to uncover how much of confidence is based on genetics and how much is influenced by our environment. I loved this book and found some of the ideas discussed applicable to anyone regardless of gender. I highly recommend the book and have provided the link below:

https://www.amazon.com/dp/006223062X?aaxitk=rnISThk91mYDzNbRRTJzFw&pd_rd_i=006223062X&pf_rd_m=ATVPDKIKX0DER&pf_rd_p=3534726502&pf_rd_s=desktop-sx-top-slot&pf_rd_t=301&pf_rd_i=the+confidence+code&hsa_cr_id=1878825940801

Continuing your education

Learning doesn't stop after high school or college graduation. In order to achieve the level of success you desire, you must develop an insatiable appetite for knowledge. In this section, I highlight some of the strategies my clients and I have utilized to achieve our goals.

Joining growth focused organizations

As discussed in the *Continuing your education* section of the book, joining a growth focused organization can be a great way to develop new skills and expand your network. I've been a part of Toastmasters for over two years and as a result I feel more confident as a public speaker. Below I've provided a list of some of the most popular growth focused organizations. Also, do some research on your own to see if there are any of these organizations in your area. Once you find one that piques your interest, commit to attending their meetings regularly. The improvement you'll see in just a short period of time can be life changing:

Public Speaking: Toastmasters
Professional: Society of Professional Hispanic Engineers, Society of Women Engineers, American Management Association, American Business Women's Association, Business Professionals of America, American Marketing Association, etc.
(For a list of more professional organizations, click the link provided here: https://jobstars.com/professional-associations-organizations/)
Sales: National Association of Sales Professionals, The Sales Association, The Sales Management Association, and the American Association of Inside Sales Professions etc.

Educational investments

Over the last three years, I've invested a significant portion of my income into educational materials, courses, books, and coaching services. I truly believe that the best investment you can make is an investment in yourself. Below, I've provided some of the educational investments I've made:

Coaching

- ☐ In May 2016, I hired Scott Howard, a phenomenal executive coach, to help me work through various work and personal goals I had set for myself. This relationship has lasted two years and has played a big role in me writing the *Millennial Playbook* series, running my first marathon, receiving various accolades at work, and much more. I interacted with Scott twice per month for one hour at a time and approached a single goal during each call.

- ☐ In November 2017, I hired Patrick Snow, a world-renowned author, professional speaker, and coach, to coach me on how to develop a profitable speaking, coaching, and author business. Over the course of the last six months, I've landed some big gigs and established myself as a legitimate speaker and seasoned professional.

Coursework

- ☐ *Insane Productivity* – Darren Hardy

- ☐ *1K on the Side* – Ramit Sethi

- ☐ *Cardone University* – Grant Cardone

Books

- ☐ *Toilet Paper Entrepreneur* by Mike Michalowicz

- ☐ *The ONE Thing* by Gary Keller and Jay Papsan

- ☐ *Money Master the Game* by Tony Robbins

- ☐ *#AskGaryVee* by Gary Vaynerchuck

- ☐ *The Entrepreneur Rollercoaster* by Darren Hardy

- ☐ *Sleep Smarter* by Shawn Stevenson

☐ *Deep Work* by Cal Newport

☐ *Shoe Dog* by Phil Knight

☐ *The Everything Store* by Brad Stone

☐ *Rock Bottom to Rock Star* by Ryan Blair

☐ *Be Obsessed or Be Average* by Grant Cardone

☐ *The 22 Immutable Laws of Marketing* by Jack Trout and Al Reis

☐ *Work Rules* by Lazlo Bock

☐ *Benjamin Franklin* by Walter Isaacson

☐ *The Millionaire Playbook* by Grant Cardone

☐ *Will It Fly* by Pat Flynn

☐ *Rework* by David Heinemeier Hansson and Jason Fried

☐ *American Icon* by Bryce G. Hoffman

☐ *Solve for Happy* by Mo Gawdat

☐ *Sell or Be Sold* by Grant Cardone

Along with these 20 titles, there are more than 40 others that were not listed. If you'd like find out more about what other books I've read and found helpful, feel free to reach out to me at recollaz@gmail.com.

As you can see, some of these materials are not even related to institutional education. Some of the best lessons I've learned have been a result of interactions with my coaches, devouring books on various subjects, and engaging with coursework provided by entrepreneurs who have experienced massive success in their life. You don't have to necessarily go back to college to get an education. Invest in a few of these methods and you'll be well on your way to becoming a well-rounded individual who will contribute a substantial amount to the world.

References

Rigoglioso, Marguerite. "Francis Flynn: If You Want Something, Ask For It." *Stanford Graduate School of Business* (2018).[1]

Johnson, David W., Roger T. Johnson, and Karl A. Smith. "Cooperative learning: Improving university instruction by basing practice on validated theory." *Journal on Excellence in University Teaching* 25.4 (2014): 1-26.[2]

Keim, Brandon. "Happiness And Sadness Spread Just Like Disease." *Wired* (2014).[3]

J Marsh, J Suttie. "5 Ways Giving Is Good for You." *Greater Good Magazine*, science-based insights for a meaningful life 13 December 2010.[4]

Ornish, Living. "Science Shows That Kindness Heals." Ed. Lydia Polgreen. 06 December 2017. <https://www.huffingtonpost.com/ornish-living/science-shows-that-kindne_1_b_6474396.html>.[5]

Gandhi, Bela. "7 dating tips to steal from Millennials." 07 June 2017. <https://www.today.com/health/how-millennials-date-today-t112431>.[6]

Keller, Gary, and Jay Papasan. The one thing: The surprisingly simple truth behind extraordinary results. *Bard Press*, 2013.[7]

Gladwell, Malcolm. *Outliers: The Story of Success*. Hachette UK, 2008.[8]

Cuddy, Amy. "Your Body Language May Shape Who You Are." TEDTalks website. (2012).[9]

Wallace, J P, et al. "Twelve Month Adherence of Adults Who Joined a Fitness Program with a Spouse vs without a Spouse." *Advances in Pediatrics.*, U.S. National Library of Medicine, Sept. 1995, www.ncbi.nlm.nih.gov/pubmed/8775648.[10]

Stafford, Tom. "Psychology: Why bad news dominates the headlines." *BBC Future*. BBC 28 (2014).[11]

Fredrickson, Barbara L. "The broaden-and-build theory of positive emotions." *Philosophical Transactions of the Royal Society B: Biological Sciences* 359.1449 (2004): 1367.[12]

Lehrer, Jonah. "Blame it on the brain." *The Wall Street Journal* (2009).[13]

Maria, Konnikova. "On the Face of It: The Psychology of Electability." The New Yorker 18 November 2013. <https://www.newyorker.com/tech/elements/on-the-face-of-it-the-psychology-of-electability>.[14]

Walen, Heather R., and Margie E. Lachman. "Social support and strain from partner, family, and friends: Costs and benefits for men and women in adulthood." *Journal of Social and Personal Relationships* 17.1 (2000): 5-30.[15]

Eisenberg, Marla E. et al. "The role of social norms and friends' influences on unhealthy weight-control behaviors among adolescent girls." *Social Science & Medicine* 60.6 (2005): 1165-1173.[16]

Crosnoe, Robert, Chandra Muller, and Kenneth Frank. "Peer context and the consequences of adolescent drinking." *Social Problems* 51.2 (2004): 288-304.[17]

Taylor, Jim. "The Power of Prime." (2009).[18]

Daniels, Aubrey. PIC – Positive Immediate Consequence. 01 November 2009. Daug Wick. <http://positioningsystems.com/blog.php?entryID=141>.[19]

Avolio, Bruce J., and William L. Gardner. "Authentic leadership development: Getting to the root of positive forms of leadership." *The Leadership Quarterly* 16.3 (2005): 315-338.[20]

Carniol, Alan. "4 Ways To Plan For A Super-Productive Day The Night Before." *Fast Company* 02 08 2016. <https://www.fastcompany.com/3056383/4-ways-to-plan-for-a-super-productive-day-the-night-before>.[21]

Starecheski, L. "Why saying is believing—the science of self-talk." *National Public Radio* (2014).[22]

Rifasggs, Ransom. "Who Reads Books?" *Mental Floss*, 2011.[23]

Keefe, John, et al. "Average Commute Times" WNYC, 2012, project.wnyc.org/commute-times-us/mobile.html#5.00/42.000/-89.500.[24]

Evans, Lisa. "Why Sharing Your Progress Makes You More Likely To Accomplish Your Goals." *Fast Company* 06 19 2015. <https://www.fastcompany.com/3047432/why-sharing-your-progress-makes-you-more-likely-to-accomplish-your-goals>.[25]

Cohen, Philip. "Mental gymnastics increase bicep strength." *New Scientist* 21 (2001).[26]

Buddhism by country. n.d. <https://en.wikipedia.org/wiki/Buddhism_by_country>.[27]

"What Are Your Values? Deciding What's Most Important in Life." Mindtools.com.[28]

Gregoire, Carolyn. "This Is Scientific Proof That Happiness Is A Choice." *The Huffington Post* (2013). [29]

Nobel, Carmen. "Reflecting on Work Improves Job Performance." *Harvard Business School Working Knowledge*, 2014.[30]

Smith, Emily Esfahani. "Social connection makes a better brain." *The Atlantic* (2013).[31]

Davidson, Lauren. "Is your daily social media usage higher than average?" *The Telegraph* 17 (2015).[32]

Galla, Brian M., and Angela L. Duckworth. "More than resisting temptation: Beneficial habits mediate the relationship between self-control and positive life outcomes." *Journal of Personality and Social Psychology* 109.3 (2015): 508.[33]

Emmons, Robert A., and Michael E. McCullough. "Counting blessings versus burdens: an experimental investigation of gratitude and subjective wellbeing in daily life." *Journal of Personality and Social Psychology* 84.2 (2003): 377.[34]

Adachi, Noel. "AAAHC Quality Roadmap 2017." *Institute for Quality Improvement*, doi:http://www.aaahc.org/Global/AAAHC%20Institute_Quality%20Roadmap/AAAHC_Quality_Roadmap_2017_FINAL.pdf.[35]

DiSalvo, David. "10 Things You Should Know About Goals." *Pharma & Healthcare* (2010).[36]

"Only Four Basic Emotions Exist, Researchers Say." 03 02 2014. <http://www.sci-news.com/othersciences/psychology/science-four-basic-emotions-01742.html>.[37]

Breines, Juliana. "The Perils of Comparing Ourselves to Others." *Psychology Today* 31.7 (2014).[38]

St John, Warren. "Sorrow So Sweet. A Guilty Pleasure in Another's Woe." *New York Times* 24 (2002).[39]

Wayment, H. A., & O'Mara, E. M. (2008). The collective and compassionate consequences of downward social comparisons. In H. A. Wayment & J. J. Bauer (Eds.), *Decade of behavior. Transcending self-interest: Psychological explorations of the quiet ego* (pp. 159-169).[40]

Washington, DC, US: American Psychological Association. Patten, Eileen, and Richard Fry. "How Millennials today compare with their grandparents 50 years ago." *Pew Research Center* 19 (2015).[41]

Sandstrom, Gillian M., and Elizabeth W. Dunn. "Social interactions and wellbeing: The surprising power of weak ties." *Personality and Social Psychology Bulletin* 40.7 (2014): 910-922.[42]

Park, Crystal L., et al. "Meaning making and psychological adjustment following cancer: the mediating roles of growth, life meaning, and restored just-world beliefs." *Journal of Consulting and Clinical Psychology* 76.5 (2008): 863.[43]

Killam, Kasley. "How to Find Meaning in Suffering." *Scientific American* (2015).[44]

Frankl, Viktor E. *Man's Search for Meaning.* Simon and Schuster, 1985.[45]

Dutton, Judy. "Make Your Bed, Change Your Life?" *Psychology Today* (2012).[46]

Duhigg, Charles. The Power of Habit: Why we do what we do in life and business. Vol. 34. No. 10. Random House, 2012.[47]

Brogaard, Berit. "Effects of Laughter on the Human Brain." *livestrong.com* 14.8 (2017).[48]

Provine, Robert R. "the science of laughter." *Psychology Today* 33.6 (2000): 58-62.[49]

Freud, Sigmund. *The Ego and the Id.* WW Norton & Company, 1962.[50]

Kuss, Daria J., and Mark D. Griffiths. "Online social networking and addiction—a review of the psychological literature." *International Journal of Environmental Research and Public Health* 8.9 (2011): 3528-3552.[51]

Kirschner, Paul A., and Aryn C. Karpinski. "Facebook® and academic performance." *Computers in Human Behavior* 26.6 (2010): 1237-1245.[52]

Steers, Mai-Ly N., Robert E. Wickham, and Linda K. Acitelli. "Seeing everyone else's highlight reels: How Facebook usage is linked to depressive symptoms." *Journal of Social and Clinical Psychology* 33.8 (2014): 701-731.[53]

Self-licensing. n.d. <https://en.wikipedia.org/wiki/Self-licensing>.[54]

Wyand, Sarah Katherine. "Are College Students Playing Hard so That They Can Drink Harder?: Examining Greek Affiliation as a Predictor of Drunkorexia." 2017 NCUR (2017).[55]

Wilcox, Keith, et al. "Vicarious goal fulfillment: When the mere presence of a healthy option leads to an ironically indulgent decision." *Journal of Consumer Research* 36.3 (2009).[56]

Hattie, John, and Helen Timperley. "The power of feedback." *Review of Educational Research* 77.1 (2007).[57]

Steiert, Stephanie. "The Bricklayers Parable." Pathways to Purpose, 2015, doi:58) http://pathways.shc.edu/wp-content/uploads/2016/12/Bricklayers-ParableActivity.pdf.[58]

Moser, Jason S., et al. "Mind your errors: Evidence for a neural mechanism linking growth mind-set to adaptive posterior adjustments." *Psychological Science* 22.12 (2011).[59]

Biography. n.d. <https://www.biography.com/people/john-logie-baird-9195738>.[60]

Lynch, John. The average American watches so much TV it's almost a full-time job. Ed. Henry Blodget. 28 06 2016. *Business Insider Inc.* 15 05 2018. <http://www.businessinsider.com/how-much-tv-do-americans-watch-2016-6>.[61]

Blaszczak-Boxe, Agata. "Too Much TV Really Is Bad for Your Brain." (2015).[62]

Neal, David T., Wendy Wood, and Aimee Drolet. "How do people adhere to goals when willpower is low? The profits (and pitfalls) of strong habits." *Journal of Personality and Social Psychology* 104.6 (2013).[63]

Wrzesniewski, Amy, et al. "Jobs, careers, and callings: People's relations to their work." *Journal of Research in Personality* 31.1 (1997).[64]

Williams, Scott. Wright State University. n.d. <http://www.wright.edu/~scott.williams/LeaderLetter/listening.htm>.[65]

Huseman, Richard C., James M. Lahiff, and John M. Penrose. *Business Communication: Strategies and Skills.* Harcourt School, 1991.[66]

Epley, Nicholas, and Erin Whitchurch. "Mirror, mirror on the wall: Enhancement in self-recognition." *Personality and Social Psychology Bulletin* 34.9 (2008): 1159-1170.[67]

Travis, Bradberry. "Why successful people are great listeners." *World Economic Forum.* 2015.[68]

Drenth, Dr. A.J. " Ego, Identity, & Ego Defensiveness." *Personality Junkie.*[69]

Schultz, Rachael. "12 Morning Tricks to Set Yourself Up For A Much Less Stressful Day." *Prevention* 2014: 3.16 may. 2018.[70]

Randler, Christoph. "The early bird really does get the worm." *Harvard Business Review* 88.7-8 (2010): 30.[71]

Kulreet Chaudhary, M.D. "Sleep and Longevity." *Doctoroz.com*, 2011. **Dr. Oz**. 3 July 2017.[72]

Jones, Jeffrey M. "In US, 40% get less than recommended amount of sleep." *Well Being* 19 (2013).[73]

Stevenson, Shawn. *Sleep Smarter.* Rodale, 2016.[74]

Winter-Hébert, Lana. "10 Benefits of Reading: Why You Should Read Every Day." *Lifehack.org* 2014: 2. **Lifehack - Help, Tips and Guidance to improve all aspects of your life**. **www.lifehack.org/articles/lifestyle/10-benefits-reading-why-you-should-read-everyday.html. 3 July 2017**.[75]

Murray, Bridget. "Writing to heal." *Monitor on Psychology* 33.6 (2002): 54.[76]

Dienstmann, Giovanni. " Scientific Benefits of Meditation-76 Things You Might be Missing Out on." *Live and Dare* (http://liveanddare. com/typesofmeditation/).[77]

Cloud, John. "Losing focus? Studies say meditation may help." *Time*. Online edition 6 (2010).[78]

Pros, Damian. "5 Reasons Why Writing Down Goals Increases the Odds of Achieving Them." Elite Daily 30 June 2015. *Elite Daily*. 5 July 2017.[79]

Smith, Dave. "7 Benefits of Morning Exercise, Plus 5 Tricks To Actually Love It (even if you hate mornings!)." Makeyourbodywork.com. **Make Your Body Work**. 3 July 2017.[80]

Davis, Jeanie Lerche. " Lose Weight with Morning Exercise." *Web MD Health News* (2010).[81]

Hillman, Charles H., Kirk I. Erickson, and Arthur F. Kramer. "Be smart, exercise your heart: exercise effects on brain and cognition." *Nature Reviews Neuroscience* 9.1 (2008): 58.[82]

"Breakfast Research & Statistics." Mrbreakfast.com. **MrBreakfast.com - All Breakfast All the Time**. 3 July 2017.[83]

Westerterp, Klaas R. "Diet induced thermogenesis." *Nutrition & Metabolism* 1.1 (2004): 5.[84]

Rice, Lori. "Benefits of a High Protein Breakfast." Fitstar.com. 8 Apr. 2014. **LIVESTRONG.COM - Simple Healthy Living | LIVESTRONG.COM**. fitstar.com/benefits-high-protein-breakfast. 3 July 2017.[85]

Amabile, Teresa M., and Steven J. Kramer. "The power of small wins." *Harvard Business Review* 89.5 (2011).[86]

"New study shows we work harder when we are happy." Warwick. *University of Warwick.* https://warwick.ac.uk/newsandevents/pressreleases/new_study_shows/. 3 July 2017.[87]

Ranganathan, Vinoth K., et al. "From mental power to muscle power—gaining strength by using the mind." *Neuropsychologia* 42.7 (2004): 944-956.[88]

Starecheski, Laura. "Why Saying Is Believing—The Science Of Self-Talk." *NPR Health* (2014).[89]

Behncke, Like. "Self-regulation: A brief review." Athletic Insight14.1 (2002). *Self-Regulation: A Brief Review - Athletic Insight.* 3 July 2017.[90]

Kross, Ethan, et al. "Self-talk as a regulatory mechanism: How you do it matters." *Journal of Personality and Social Psychology* 106.2 (2014): 304.[91]

Settanni, Michele, and Davide Marengo. "Sharing feelings online: Studying emotional wellbeing via automated text analysis of Facebook posts." *Frontiers in Psychology* 6 (2015): 1045.[92]

Conversano, Ciro, et al. "Optimism and its impact on mental and physical wellbeing." *Clinical Practice and Epidemiology in Mental Health:* CP & EMH 6 (2010): 25.[93]

Krause, Neal, and Christopher G. Ellison. "Forgiveness by God, forgiveness of others, and psychological wellbeing in late life." *Journal for the Scientific Study of Religion* 42.1 (2003).[94]

Powell, Vania Bitencourt, et al. "Changing core beliefs with trial-based cognitive therapy may improve quality of life in social phobia: a randomized study." *Revista Brasileira de Psiquiatria* 35.3 (2013).[95]

Seidman, Gwendolyn. "Are Narcissists Nastier to Their Romantic Partners?" *Psychology Today* (2017).[96]

MacLean, Katherine A., et al. "Intensive meditation training improves perceptual discrimination and sustained attention." *Psychological Science* 21.6 (2010).[97]

Randler, Christoph. "The early bird really does get the worm." *Harvard Business Review* 88.7-8 (2010): 30.[98]

Ferrari, Joseph R. et al. "Exploring the time preferences by procrastinators: Night or day, which is the one?" *European Journal of Personality* 11.3 (1997).[99]

Gawande, Atul, and John Bedford Lloyd. *The Checklist Manifesto: How to Get Things Right.* Vol. 200. New York: Metropolitan Books, 2010.[100]

Dictionary, Merriam-Webster. "Merriam-Webster." *Google Scholar* (1983).[101]

Teresa, M. Amabile, and J. Kramer Steven. *The Power of Small Wins*. 2011.[102]

Shaffer, Joyce. "Neuroplasticity and positive psychology in clinical practice: A review for combined benefits." *Psychology* 3.12 (2012).[103]

Ranganathan, Vinoth K., et al. "From mental power to muscle power—gaining strength by using the mind." *Neuropsychologia* 42.7 (2004).[104]

"Frequently Monitoring Progress Toward Goals Increases Chance of Success." ***American Psychological Association***. www.apa.org, 28 October, 2015. ***http://www.apa.org/news/press/releases/2015/10/progress-goals.aspx***. 3 June 2017.[105]

Fogel, Alan. "Emotional and Physical Pain Activate Similar Brain Regions." *Psychology Today* 19 (2012).[106]

Poldrack, Russell A. "What Is Loss Aversion?." 2014: 2. <u>What Is Loss Aversion? - Scientific American</u>. https://www.scientific american.com/article/what-is-loss-aversion/. 3 Jan. 2017.[107]

Holiday, Ryan. *Ego is the Enemy*. Profile Books Ltd, 2017.[108]

Huang, K., Yeomans, M., Brooks, A. W., Minson, J., & Gino, F. (2017). "It doesn't hurt to ask: Question-asking increases liking." *Journal of Personality and Social Psychology*. doi: 10.1037/pspi0000097[109]